Language across the curric
four case studies

SCHOOLS COUNCIL WORKING PAPER 67

Language across the curriculum: four case studies

the report of the Schools Council
Language across the Curriculum Project

IRENE ROBERTSON

Edited with an Introduction by RICHARD CHOAT
Foreword by MICHAEL MARLAND

Methuen Educational

First published 1980 for the Schools Council
160 Great Portland Street, London W1N 6LL
by Methuen Educational
11 New Fetter Lane, London EC4P 4EE

Printed in Great Britain by
Richard Clay (The Chaucer Press) Ltd
Bungay, Suffolk

British Library Cataloguing in Publication Data

Schools Council Language across the Curriculum Project
Language across the curriculum: four case studies.
(Schools Council. Working Papers; 67 ISSN 0533–1668).
1. English language – Study and teaching – Great Britain – Case studies
  I. Title   II. Robertson, Irene
     420′.7′1042   LB1576

ISBN 0-423-50790-7

Contents

Foreword

Of all the recommendations of *A Language for Life*, the Report of the Bullock Committee, the reasonable-sounding, apparently straightforward and certainly cheap ones embodying the idea of 'language across the curriculum' have proved the most difficult to implement.

Most recommendations of committees of inquiry are addressed to certain points in the system, maybe certain teachers in schools, and it is clear who should consider them and how they might be implemented. Bullock's central recommendation, however, was addressed to all! More than that, it involved school organization, curriculum planning, learning resources policies, and the details and spirit of every teacher's work with every pupil. Even well-disposed schools have found this extremely difficult. After all, the call for 'across the curriculum' planning runs counter to the vertical, separate-subject tradition of syllabus planning. It is far more than the 'integration' of a group of similar subjects, and demands a fundamental consideration of what is being taught and how the teaching process is being developed.

The Schools Council's English Committee had by 1977 formulated proposals concerned with writing (Writing across the Curriculum 11–16) and reading (The Effective Use of Reading) across the curriculum; it was felt that the next useful step would be to commission a study of secondary schools which had already gone some way towards implementing their own language policies across the curriculum.

This report by Irene Robertson uses the perspective of a classroom teacher, linguist and sociologist to observe sympathetically, but coolly, the efforts of schools trying in their various ways and from different developmental positions a whole-school policy. It was not the aim of the project to discover 'the answers', for in our dispersed and varied education system there are no readily generalizable solutions. It does, however, reveal the nature of the problems, and describes vividly the complexity of the tension between autonomy and coherence in our schools.

Bullock's call for 'a language policy across the curriculum' is a call for a new coherence of school management, and a new partnership between teachers, working separately, in different contexts and in different styles – but using common approaches. In any other country the aim would have been translated outside the school into a series of mandatory instructions or curricular guides. We leave it to the teachers in the schools to work out, and this report takes us into four schools struggling, sometimes but not always with outside help, towards that new coherence. As we read, we share the difficulties and the achievements, and we come out better placed to develop a language policy in our own schools.

MICHAEL MARLAND
Chairman, Schools Council English Committee

Acknowledgements

I would like to offer thanks to the heads and staffs of the schools I visited during the project. I am particularly grateful to those teachers and pupils who let me visit their lessons and tape them at work. Interpretations of what I heard and saw are my responsibility and my judgements may not necessarily be shared by the teachers and pupils concerned.

I wish to thank all the schools for giving me permission to reproduce worksheets, policy statements and children's work.

My especial thanks go to the project's consultative committee; Miss Helen Carter of the Schools Council; Victor Burgess, London Borough of Harrow; and Mick Hornsby, The Geoffrey Chaucer School, London SE1.

I. R.

Introduction

This book, the report of the Schools Council Language across the Curriculum Project, is the outcome of an investigation carried out by Irene Robertson in 1977/78. Four schools which had made some progress in developing a language across the curriculum policy were studied. Ms. Robertson traced the history of language policy work in each school and, in the course of the short visits, concentrated on the organizational aspects of school life which helped to bring a language policy into being, and on how far that policy had affected classroom practice. The reader will find details of the methods she employed on p. 22. A summary of the trends in educational thinking and research (including the publication of *A Language for Life* – the 'Bullock Report'[1]) which fostered the current widespread interest in her topic can be found on p. 19ff. The purpose of this introduction is to draw together common threads in the four case studies and explore the implications of some of the views expressed in the project report.

The case studies are addressed primarily to teachers with an interest in the ways in which language can be used in the complementary processes of teaching and learning. With this audience (including headteachers, heads of departments, subject specialists and trainees) in mind, the case studies are organized more as an illustrative handbook of practical ideas than as a social scientific research report. Each study includes a sketch of the successes and difficulties encountered in putting the new work into practice and substantial extracts from documents produced within the school. The accounts of lessons clarify some of the implications for classroom teaching, using extracts from tape-recordings and children's written work. Interspersed among these records of the growth and flowering of curriculum innovation are Ms. Robertson's comments and analysis.

A recurring and central theme of the report, which helps to uncover the preconditions for a successful language policy in schools, is that *A Language for Life*'s invitation to teachers to reflect on the role of language 'in other areas of the curriculum than English' and to 'create in the classroom an environment which encourages a wide range of language uses'[2] is a recommendation for a thoroughgoing reassessment of the whole school curriculum. A call to consider radical change in teaching methods and to assess critically the objectives which conventional wisdom associates with those methods is bound to make teachers uneasy that criticism of their present practice is implied. At School 1, for example, teachers initially preferred to work at language-related curriculum reform within specific subject areas rather than by tackling the more daunting general issues. A small exploratory exercise to find out what writing was being done at School 2 generated hostility rather than provoking constructive discussion. There was also some concern in Schools 1 and 3 at the involvement of pupils in looking at current courses and searching for new ways of working.

It would be unfair to attribute this initial resistance simply to the conservatism of teachers, their concern to maintain an entrenched position within the authority structure of the school or even the threat posed by a development which would undermine professional security based on a mastery of particular content areas and styles of presentation familiar through long-established habit. Part of the difficulty encountered in opening up language work seems to be a result of poor communication within staffrooms and a justifiable anxiety that one will be told how to teach by language policy committees, members of the English Department or local authority advisers. When teachers were able to observe each others' lessons in a relaxed, co-operative manner, draw on ideas from other departments in developing their own teaching or quietly work on their own tapes of lessons and questions to pupils, many positive ideas and useful experiments emerged in a fairly short space of time.

The report makes clear that the burden of language across the curriculum work has fallen more heavily on teachers than on agencies outside the school. Originally a grassroots movement, particularly among English teachers, language and learning – despite the official imprimatur of the Bullock Report and the subsequent keenness of local education authorities to be seen to be doing something relevant – has still largely remained a school-based enterprise. As Ms. Robertson indicates, even though *A Language for Life* advocates embodying responsibility for language and learning 'in the organisational structure of the school'[3] it tends to shy away from achieving this through provision of substantial DES and LEA support and modification of the national examination system and the hierarchical structure of schools. This wider context influences all moves for curriculum change. The sections of the present report dealing with external support to schools do not make encouraging reading. Despite the excellent and effective work made possible at School 3 by links between the school and a member of the staff of the local authority teachers' centre, one gets the general impression of a token provision of adviser posts spread thinly over local authorities' schools, providing their incumbents with a heavy workload that may include responsibility for several other areas as well as language across the curriculum. The one-off courses or talks about language and learning that have been organized can spark interest amongst teachers, but the lack of follow-through (cf. the unavailablity of funds for in-service Open University courses at School 1) can lead to disappointment and frustration. As the National Union of Teachers' commentary on the Bullock Report points out *vis-à-vis* in-service education, 'there is little evidence of increased provision overall'[4]. It may be that new initiatives, such as the joint DES/local authority short courses, will bear fruit, but in an era of educational cutbacks one cannot be optimistic.

Other constraints affected language and learning work to different degrees in the schools studied. School 4 was particularly badly hit by the teacher shortage and high level of staff turnover during the immediate post-Bullock period, and its recovery is now likely to be made more difficult by the effect of financial stringencies on the provision of materials and resources. The difficulty of experimenting with the curriculum on the basis of a school's evaluation of its educational needs while simultaneously preparing pupils for nationally standardized examinations was felt keenly at School 2 and featured in the awareness of staff at School 3. Surprisingly, in view of the amount of publicity language across the curriculum has received in the educational media, many teachers in the selected schools seem to have had, at first, only the vaguest notion of *A Language for Life*'s recommendations and some degree of suspicion that it was, after all, just another educational fad.

Against this background the achievements of individual schools documented in the report appear particularly impressive. Where successes have come about the persistence of those with some formal responsibility for language-linked curriculum development (the deputy heads at Schools 1 and 2, the language policy committees at Schools 3 and 4) emerges as a significant factor. This is partly because they are able to help out enthusiastic subject teachers with timetabling, secretarial assistance, materials, etc., and partly because they act as a reference point linking staff, so that when ideas dry up, or when joint action with other departments is needed, language policy work can continue through their supplying a focus of interest or a forum for discussion. An individual or committee with sufficient influence to make recommendations to all staff in a school or give decisive guidance is well situated both to take up language policy suggestions from staff and to convince those who might resist innovation as an irrelevant imposition. Some of the hesitations and false starts in School 4's language work, for example, can be attributed to the lack of a committed central figure.

The ways in which school language policy committees started work, surveying language practices, looking at teaching styles, coming to realize what language work was about for them and conveying that understanding to colleagues, is best gathered from a detailed reading of the separate studies. A number of comments on the most fascinating aspect of the report – the description and analysis of lessons – are appropriate here, however. Ms. Robertson uses several transcripts of teacher–pupil and pupil–pupil talk to illustrate the alternative ways of working which a perspective on language and learning makes possible. They show most convincingly the sustained, reflective and judicious work that children can do in puzzling out together the ramifications of a problem when their beliefs, judgements, culture and language are used as the basis for attaining new knowledge. At the core of the departure from traditional 'talk and chalk' teaching which these lessons exemplify is a viewpoint which, as James Britton acutely brings out in his foreword to *Teaching for Literacy*,[5] is disguised by *A Language for Life*'s attempt to be dispassionate and ecumenical with regard to the intellectual factions within the Bullock Committee's membership, split between 'those who believe in carefully constructed linear programmes, buttressed by claims for sequence, system and structure, and those who believe that development in language can only be achieved by working in a much more flexible and open-ended way'. Certainly the inspiration for much of the new language across the curriculum work does not derive from the view, which has its roots in Piaget and the British tradition of empirical psychology, that all children learn in essentially the same way via a sequence of stages such that mastery of one set of abilities must always precede mastery of the next, more sophisticated, set. One problem with this approach is that it is difficult to identify these stages.[6] From the point of view of teachers presented with theoretical definitions of stages or books and exercises supposedly appropriate to a given stage, when a child fails to perform as expected at a particular point the temptation is to regard him or her as deficient and fit only for relegation to earlier-stage material and remedial treatment. By encouraging a view of learners as passive receivers who have only to be cued into activity by materials appropriate to their stage of development and to practice with them, this approach neglects the variety of problems a child may have in interpreting material and generating an appropriate response. It also ignores the fact of linguistic and cultural diversity amongst pupils who may respond differently to oral or written stimuli because they have different expectations about its linguistic or social purpose. An alternative conception, which sees linguistic behaviour as a social rather than a psychological artefact, draws on anthropology, interactional sociology and sociolinguistics for its theoretical foundations.

In the light of this rough contrast Ms. Robertson's criticism of the sequentially organized single-answer reading workshop used in School 4 (see p. 139) and her reservations about 'teaching children skills' (p. 58) fit into a pattern. A perspective which recognizes the elaborateness and subtlety of what children already know and can do with language is more likely to lead to a reorganization of methods and materials, to attempts to get children to explain their misunderstandings or to become authentically involved in observation, discovery and the weighing of evidence than one which regards a child's performance on a worksheet or test as a neutral index of some underlying ability. This may go some way to explaining why innovations such as integrated studies, mixed-ability teaching and small-group discussion tend to go hand in hand with language across the curriculum and the constructive attempt to evaluate resources and approaches such as worksheets, lectures and note-making. Admitting the validity and coherence of a child's thought and language as opposed to treating it as an immature or incomplete version of an adult competence will also tend to redress the power imbalance between teachers and pupils, as the head at School 1 recognized in his paper on discipline (see p. 31). This stance is compatible with a belief in the productive potential of letting pupils take control of their own learning either as historians assessing primary evidence and imaginatively involved in the events they study (Humanities at School 1, History at School 3), as mathematicians inventing notations, taking on and generalizing problems (Mathematics at School 1) or as speculative botanists (Science at School 2).

Time and again in the studies examples are provided of teachers whose interest in pupils' and their own use of language develops and becomes a practical concern in lessons simply through taking up a new idea on a small scale and thinking hard about the results (see, for example, the sections on prediction and sequencing in Schools 1 and 2, and on small-group talk in Home Economics at School 3). Asking questions about the function of a language activity – silent reading, group talk, writing plays, inventing a mathematical notation – involves asking what precisely a pupil is learning and how a new accomplishment will be expressed in his or her school activities. As Ms. Robertson emphasizes, the result of this conscious reflection on classroom teaching in an attempt to move away from unthinking, stereotypical instruction will not always be the abandoning of 'traditional' activities such as whole-class discussion led by a teacher. It is the fit between teaching purposes and the conduct of teaching which is important rather than the uncritical espousal of 'traditional' or 'progressive' dogma. One of the strengths of language across the curriculum is that it encourages the speculation that children need and use language for a great range of purposes and that many of these modes can be exploited by teachers leading them through educational tasks.

A reader may well turn to this report for advice about which educational writers and thinkers would be most useful for someone coming to language policy for the first time. The most influential and best-known works are those of James Britton and Douglas Barnes.[7] These writers have argued

    i that to examine learning we have to examine language, to make language visible, rather than leave it transparent and ignore it. Learning happens in the language interactions that are generated in lessons, not in the transmission of information into pupils' heads, with language as the neutral tool for achieving this;

    ii that this will involve looking at the language of pupil and teacher, and that of textbook and worksheet; and

    iii that teachers will come to respect pupils' language because they will recognize it as (necessarily) a key resource for learning, and will come to a critical awareness of their own language in the process.

Other writers have contributed significantly to work on language and learning. Some of the most influential publications are described in the Further Reading section on p. 172.

The present report's discussion of technical and scientific language (pp. 85, 88, 113 and 147) provides a useful antidote to an assumption – often loosely associated with an enthusiasm for 'progressive' teaching – that children's everyday language (particularly forms claimed as typical of the working class) is a complete and adequate vehicle for 'school knowledge'. It is clear, however, that the connection between speech and knowledge is so close that entering into new knowledge, acquiring new concepts and learning how to employ them are linguistic activities which open up new realms of discourse – new ways of talking or writing which reflect the change in the learner. To be sure, mystifying children with a mass of difficult and alien terminology will impede the acquisition of scientific ideas or technical abilities, but one needs to remember that someone who has grasped the idea of, say, 'evaporation' has done more than learnt that it means roughly the same as 'drying out'. Understanding evaporation involves entering a conceptual universe in which a repertoire of contrasts (between liquids, vapours and gases, for example) and associations (with boiling, distillation, freezing) is expressed in new uses of language.

We must remember that we have, as yet, no comprehensive theory of which language varieties fulfil which functions for which speakers, or how exactly these distinctions can be put to educational use. The writings mentioned above and in the Further Reading section do not claim to be a substitute for the exploratory work which this book reports. The reader could do worse, as indeed the P E teacher from School 3 shows, than pick up note-pad and tape-recorder to start his or her own action research into language across the curriculum.

RICHARD CHOAT

References

1. Department of Education and Science, *A Language for Life*: Report of the Committee of Inquiry appointed by the Secretary of State for Education and Science under the Chairmanship of Sir Alan Bullock FBA [The Bullock Report], HMSO, 1975.
2. *A Language for Life*, p. 188.
3. *A Language for Life*, p. 529.
4. *A Language for Life: NUT's Commentary on the Bullock Report*, National Union of Teachers, 1976.
5. F. Davis and R. Parker (eds.), *Teaching for Literacy: Reflections on the Bullock Report*, Ward Lock Educational, 1978.
6. cf. the article by Gareth Matthews in G. Vesey (ed.), *Communication and Understanding*, Harvester Press, 1977.
7. J. Britton, *Language and Learning*, Allen Lane, 1970 (also available in Penguin); J. Britton *et al.*, *The Development of Writing Abilities (11–18)* (Schools Council Research Studies), Macmillan Education, 1975; D. Barnes, *From Communication to Curriculum*, Penguin, 1979; D. Barnes, J. Britton and H. Rosen, *Language, the Learner and the School*, Penguin, revised edition 1971.

I. The case studies: background, aims and approach

Background

The four case studies which form the bulk of this book have their origin in the publication, in February 1975, of *A Language for Life* – the report of a committee of inquiry chaired by Sir Alan (now Lord) Bullock. Set up in 1972 by Mrs Margaret Thatcher, then Secretary of State for Education, the committee's brief was to investigate and make recommendations on three topics in relation to schools:

(*a*) all aspects of teaching the use of English, including reading, writing, and speech;
(*b*) how present practice might be improved and the role that initial and in-service training might play;
(*c*) to what extent arrangements for monitoring the general level of attainment in these skills can be introduced or improved.[1]

The way the committee interpreted this task and set about the collation of research findings, the sifting of evidence from individuals and institutions and a comprehensive survey of English teaching, clearly showed awareness of 'the great public interest' in the topics under study and of a number of recent development in educational thinking.

The inclusion of topic (*c*) in the brief resulted partly from a sense amongst educators that too little was known about the process of reading, the needs of the reader and 'reading standards', partly from a generalized (and politically popular) concern that the 'three Rs' – particularly reading – should be kept up to scratch by schools. The committee found that 'there is no firm statistical base for comparison of present-day standards of reading with those of before the war . . . it is questionable whether there is anything to be gained from attempting it' (Conclusion 10) and commented that, by the age of 15, to some extent 'reading ability has outstripped the available tests' (Section 2.34), although there was some evidence of a lack of improvement in poor readers from within the working class (Section 2.25). The Assessment of Performance Unit, established by the Department of Education and Science in 1974, continues to respond to this concern in the light of the committee's Principal Recommendation 1: 'A system of monitoring should be introduced which will employ new instruments to assess a wider range of attainments than has been attempted in the past and allow new criteria to be established for the definition of literacy.'

The open-ended tone of this prescription underlines 'the important principle that reading must be seen as part of a child's general language development and not as a discrete skill which can be considered in isolation from it' (Introduction, p. xxxi). Approaches which see reading in terms of building up successively more subtle responses to the printed word recognize – in using ideas such as 'interrogation of a text' – the variety of experiences readers bring to texts in order to understand and learn. Many of the instances described in the present case studies highlight moments when what a pupil knows, is interested in or can already do is harnessed to a task so that intelligent reading becomes an integral part of moving on in learning.

The second strand in the committee's thinking, which prompted them to say, 'We have, in fact, interpreted our brief as language in education . . .' (Introduction, p. xxxi), was a recognition that speaking, reading, writing and related linguistic processes are instrumental in all areas of learning, that 'language learning' and 'learning a subject' are complementary, symbiotic developments. Here the work of Douglas Barnes at Leeds University and of the cluster of teachers and educationalists centred around Harold Rosen, Nancy Martin and James Britton of the London University Institute of Education was obviously influential. Douglas Barnes's paper[2] had drawn attention, using taped conversations of actual lessons, to the importance of talk in the secondary school across a range of subjects. The London Institute team's framework for describing varieties of mature language use – especially in writing[3] – had displayed some of the different communicative functions of language and suggested that 'expressive' speech had been neglected as an avenue into other language activities. It also served to stress that the linguistic talents a pupil possesses or can develop do not fall simply into the slots provided by school subject disciplines and are thus not the exclusive property of this or that department. These theories encouraged the realization that a learner's everyday ability to tell stories, banter, joke, question, explain and so on can all provide means for developing knowledge and understanding.

At the same time as educationalists were becoming more aware of the complexity of how learners use language, sociolinguists were coming to recognize the importance of the shared social context of language use for their own studies. Michael Halliday's view that learning a language is 'learning how to mean'[4] and an increasing emphasis on the variation of language across cultures and contexts[5] are both examples of this trend. The committee's Recommendation 133 recognizes this interest by saying: 'Linguistics and other specialist studies of language have a considerable contribution to make to the teaching of English, and they should be used to emphasise the inseparability of language and the human situation.' Underlying these quite diverse viewpoints on language and learning is a common assumption that language – oral and written – is primarily a device by which a speaker or writer communicates his or her ideas, intentions and feelings to a listener/hearer who must actively construct meaning from the speech or text.

In the six pages (Chapter 12) which *A Language for Life* devotes explicitly to language across the curriculum ('the role of language in other areas of the curriculum than English': Section 12.1) the committee briefly surveys the implications of this perspective for a teacher's assessment of his or her own language, pupil talk and study skills, recognizing that 'For language to play its full role as a means of learning, the teacher must create in the classroom an environment which encourages a wide range of language uses.' One is left in no doubt of the depth of that recognition by the report's Principal Recommendation 4:

Each school should have an organised policy for language across the curriculum, establishing every teacher's involvement in language and reading development throughout the years of schooling.

This is supported by other detailed recommendations, including:

89 There should be certain commonly agreed approaches to the teaching of reading as part of the school's policy for development of language across the curriculum.

190 The role of the head in the teaching of English is of the greatest importance, and he is uniquely placed to encourage a policy of language across the curriculum.

138 In the secondary school, all subject teachers need to be aware of:
 (i) the linguistic processes by which their pupils acquire information and understanding, and the implications for the teacher's own use of language;
 (ii) the reading demands of their own subjects and ways in which the pupils can be helped to meet them.

139 To bring about this understanding every secondary school should develop a policy for language across the curriculum. The responsibility for this policy should be embodied in the organisational structure of the school.

Since the publication of the committee's report many people have come to appreciate it, in the words of Reg Prentice – the Education Secretary to whom it was presented – as 'an authoritative statement which will be of value as a basis for further discussion and development for many years to come' (Foreword, p. iii).

There has already been much discussion. A *Times Educational Supplement* survey entitled 'Bullock Plus One', published in February 1976, revealed that 33 547 teachers had attended conferences on the report, more of which have since been organized by hard-pressed LEA advisers, teachers' centres, HMIs from the DES English Inspectorate and teachers themselves. There has also been some development. The production of recommendations for implementing the Bullock Report as a whole or language across the curriculum in particular has become an educational cottage industry of modest proportions.[6] Some pupils can even talk blithely of 'having done Bullock work'. However, at the moment there is a lack of basic information about what has been done in schools and classrooms, which might give teachers a guide to the practical steps they could take to embody a language across the curriculum policy 'in the organisational structure of the school'. It was this gap that the Schools Council Language across the Curriculum project set out to narrow.

Scope and methods of the project

In spring 1977 the Schools Council approved a proposal for a one-year, small-scale project to make case studies of schools which had gone some way towards implementing a language across the curriculum policy. I was asked to act as project director and a consultative committee, chaired by Colin Harrison, was formed to guide and advise me. My first job as project director was to consult HMIs, advisers and colleagues, who together provided me with a list of some twenty possible schools to study.

I chose schools from several parts of the country and types of area. They were not in any sense statistically typical, but I hope the accounts of their work give an inkling of the different ways a language policy can develop in a variety of circumstances. It is a regret of mine, and a serious omission from the case studies, that I have not been able to include a school that had an extensive population from diverse racial and cultural backgrounds. School 4 had the most significant multi-ethnic population, but at the time of my case-study visit it was only just beginning to consider its particular responsibilities towards the different minorities. This is not to say that their needs had hitherto been ignored, but rather that their chief apparent need, a standard of basic literacy, was one shared with the white British children. Other similar schools may have made more progress in multi-cultural language and learning in the light of developing L E A policies.

I set out to consider two distinguishable yet related aspects of language across the curriculum in a school: as a feature of school organization and policy, and as it influenced teachers at work in their classrooms. I also wanted to look at the connection between these two aspects.

I started each case study by making one or two preliminary visits to a school to see if there was indeed enough of a language policy at work to make such a study worth while. I would talk with the teachers where work I was interested in was going on and devise a timetable that would allow me the opportunity to see teachers in lessons, have some time to talk and, where appropriate, enable me to join sessions of language working parties. I also made a point of talking with whoever had the best overview of language and learning in each school to collect background information and documentation on the school's work.

The preliminaries settled, I visited each school for a block of time lasting three weeks, a period largely determined by how much overall time I had available and by the upsets to a school's life of things like beginnings of new terms, Christmas and examinations. In tracing the progress of language across the curriculum within a school, I tried not simply to chronicle events but to focus on the place and status of the work in the school and particularly upon support given it by the head. In one of the schools reported on here, and much more acutely in another school I visited, the head's lack of interest and understanding of language across the curriculum meant that the considerable work put into it by teaching staff was failing to graft itself onto the life of the school. School 2 had the reverse of this problem as the head was convinced of the importance of language and learning but had something of an uphill struggle to muster the support of large numbers of his staff.

In all the schools I visited, investigating language policy work meant looking at language policy working parties (sometimes referred to as Bullock committees or language and learning committees). I asked how members were chosen or elected and how a committee reported back to other staff. I also looked at the jobs that each working party undertook. All of them did some kind of survey. In some cases the object was not just to gather information but to present staff with evidence that language was everyone's concern and could raise interesting questions. Generally a survey seemed to be of greater value to the people conducting it than to anyone else. In School 2, for instance, making the survey framework and deciding how to characterize types of writing was itself an educative activity for those taking part. On the other hand, many people presented with evidence of a school's language problems will be angry rather than grateful, as the hostility aroused at School 2 shows. Nevertheless it may well be beneficial for people to be upset because they have been told something, rather than happy but ignorant. Other words of caution about surveys I include in the account of School 3 (p. 99). The survey carried out in School 4 was written up as its language policy document – a survey of present practice and recommendations for future work rather than an account of achievement. I comment in that case study on the place of written policies. This was the only school of the ones I scrutinized which had a policy document. At the other schools language policy committes were producing reports and working papers – an indication that language across the curriculum was still seen very much as 'work in progress'.

Finding out about the organizational and policy side of a school's language across the curriculum work involved my joining the routine life of the school: going to committee meetings with notebook and tape-recorder, talking informally in staffrooms and pubs, and drawing on the evidence of those staff members who seemed most reliable and informative. Piecing together how the work had developed in a school, on the basis of fallible memories and whatever documents were available, left me – like any ethnographer or local historian – with a necessarily partial and limited impression but, usually, a coherent one none the less.

In visiting lessons a number of difficult choices had to be made. Overall I wanted to be able to report on as many curricular areas as possible. I knew that it would not be possible to represent all the areas in any one school, firstly because I would not have the time to fit everything in and secondly because not every subject would have modified its work in response to the language and learning debate. I chose departments which were taking part in language across the curriculum activities in their school, and which felt that they had something to show for their work. The teachers whose work is described in the report represent a range of teaching experience and a variety of positions with respect to the language across the curriculum discussions in their schools. Some of them were confident and articulate about the debate as it applied to their subject (the mathematics teacher in School 1, for instance); some of them were experimenting with curriculum development in language and learning terms (see 'Enquiry' in School 1). One teacher (of PE at School 3) was just beginning to consider the relevance of it all to her subject and was doing her own language survey for her department. There were teachers like the woodwork/metalwork teacher in School 4 who had felt his own way along intuitively but now also needed a framework in order to articulate what he had achieved. There were teachers like the Head of History in School 1 who with her department had developed her curriculum via a consideration of skills, and only recently had begun to see the connections between the investigations she was encouraging and language and learning.

Not believing in the possibility of myself (or anyone) being able to make an objective account of, or get a total picture of, a lesson, I was not unduly burdened by worries about my presence as an outsider influencing the lessons I saw, and so invalidating what I reported. However, I did want teacher, pupils and myself to feel at ease while I was in the classroom, so I made tape-recordings inconspicuously but without concealment and would make notes (of what was on the blackboard, what had been said or done, and so on) while pupils were occupied with their own writing. I waited for children to involve me in a lesson, which they usually did as some sort of teacher help. When I wanted to join a group at work I would answer their questions by explaining that I was interested in what happened in lessons, how people learnt and what happened when pupils were left to get on with work in groups. This seemed, usually, to be taken at face value. Two girls I had taped working together in a humanities lesson certainly appreciated the advantages of this technique over simulations conducted outside the classroom. They made a tape commenting on the recording of their work which included:

SARA It's good I think that that lady did it in a lesson instead of having two people sit down as though they were working because . . .
LOUISE I tend to forget.
SARA Because half the things I've said on that tape, if I'd known – I'd literally forgotten the tape was on.
LOUISE You couldn't tell it was on.

The lessons I describe are not intended to be read as prescriptions for good practice or models to be adopted uncritically (indeed some of the lessons are quite strongly, though I hope not unsympathetically, criticized). They are offered simply as illustrations and interpretations of the kinds of question that language and learning can raise in various subject areas.

What I looked at and reported about lessons was, obviously enough, determined by my own understanding of language across the curriculum. I looked a lot at talk, particularly the talk of pupils at work together, listening for the ways in which they undertook their learning and trying to appreciate how they had been helped or hindered by the ways in which the teacher had set up their work. I listened, too, for teacher interventions which might facilitate learning and its expression in further talk. The value of talk – which takes up far more lesson time than reading or writing – still seems to be underestimated, perhaps because it doesn't come in markable chunks like essays, reports or poems. I took note of reading, and was interested to see if reading was recognized as an activity involving interpretation of a text on the basis of particular interests and purposes rather than a decoding exercise aimed at uncovering the one message or answer hidden in the form of words. Again, I listened for teacher interventions in that reading. I looked at writing to see how it related to the other language processes. Were pupils encouraged to shape their own writing or were they asked to write to previously given formulae? Were different kinds of writing encouraged or did writing in a particular subject always involve one limited set of activities, as if learning that subject consisted of just those activities?

Once again I was using my own understanding to interpret what I saw: I was going into classrooms with a knowledge of their general nature, but also taking with me a particular set of concerns which would focus my responses to what I saw and heard. The results of that focusing form the case studies which follow.

References

1. Department of Education and Science, *A Language for Life*: Report of the Committee of Inquiry appointed by the Secretary of State for Education and Science under the Chairmanship of Sir Alan Bullock F B A [The Bullock Report], H M S O, 1975, p. xxxi.
2. D. Barnes, 'Language in the secondary classroom', in D. Barnes *et al.*, *Language, the Learner and the School*, Penguin, revised edition 1971.
3. Incorporated in Chapter 6 of J. Britton *et al.*, *The Development of Writing Abilities (11–18)* (Schools Council Research Studies), Macmillan Education, 1975.
4. M. A. K. Halliday, *Learning How to Mean: Explorations in the Development of Language*, Edward Arnold, 1975.
5. See, for example, B. Bernstein, *Class, Codes and Control*, Vol. 1, Paladin, 1973; and P. Trudgill, *Accent, Dialect and the School*, Edward Arnold, 1975.
6. See, for example, M. Marland, *Language across the Curriculum: the Implementation of the Bullock Report in the Secondary School*, Heinemann, 1977; E. Hunter-Grundin and H. U. Grundin,

Reading: Implementing the Bullock Report, Ward Lock Educational for UKRA, 1978; and F. Davis and R. Parker (eds.), *Teaching for Literacy: Reflections on the Bullock Report*, Ward Lock Educational, 1978.

II. Case study 1

School 1 is an eight-form entry, 11–18, mixed comprehensive school of some 1400 pupils standing about eight miles east of one of the Midlands' expanding cities. The school reorganized along comprehensive lines in 1971; it was formerly a small mixed secondary-modern school. Because of its rural nature – the school is sited in a small market town that serves as a commuter 'dormitory' for the city as well as providing some local light industry – the school has a large number of primary feeder schools. Consequently, a high percentage of children is bussed to and from school each day.

Though the school is relatively near the facilities of the city, it is nevertheless quite remote from it as far as the children are concerned. They talk about their rare excursions to town as something of an adventure.

The school has strongly developed pastoral and house systems, and is based academically on six major faculties: English; Mathematics; Science; Humanities (including Modern Languages); Creative Arts, Craft and Design; and P E and Games. It enjoys excellent facilities, with suites of classrooms and work areas corresponding to the faculty organization, a concert hall, a drama workshop and a separate music block. The extensive sports facilities are shared jointly by school and local community; the sports centre was, in fact, one of the first joint-use centres in the country.

Though it is difficult, if not misleading, to attach labels to schools, it is fair to say that School 1 has something of a reputation as far as curriculum development is concerned, particularly through Mode III O-level examinations, involvement in Schools Council projects, pioneering areas such as health education and work experience – amongst which the work done in relation to language and learning is currently the most exciting.

Developing a language policy

The story of School 1's language work is particularly interesting because it provides examples of almost all the ways I have come across of approaching a language policy and, inevitably, illustrations of how approaches may go right or wrong. I made two visits to the school, in May 1977 and March 1978, and during the second visit was able to check on how the first initiatives had grown into a substantial and diverse set of courses and activities.

In the first stage of the school's language and learning work (from about November 1975 to March 1976) the concern was one which became very familiar to me as I did successive case studies: how to involve and get the interest and support of as many staff as possible. A new deputy head with responsibility for the curriculum had been appointed in September 1975. An explicit part of his brief was to develop language policy in the school. The head had seen this as a measure of the school's commitment to 'Bullock work', commenting that 'you have to show institutionally that you believe in a thing – it was important that one of the deputies was given the job'. This kind of appointment is one sign that language is being taken seriously as a curriculum issue which will be allowed to influence the wider organizational structures of the school, so that, for example, recommendations coming from language policy discussion will have a fair chance of being taken up, given resources and implemented. It goes beyond the thinking of the Bullock Report's Recommendation 139, which, although urging that responsibility for language and learning should be embodied in the organizational structure of the school, seems to see that structure as to do with fostering the understanding of 'the linguistic processes by which ... pupils acquire information and understanding, and the implications for the teacher's own use of language' (Recommendation 138) rather than with the conditions that can achieve curriculum change.

Very early on in the school's language policy programme a full staff meeting was held followed by a full staff conference addressed by outside speakers. The staff felt that the chief value of the meetings was the opportunity they provided to talk to colleagues from other departments within their school. Big day conferences, meetings for single schools or groups of schools, and the visits of outside speakers are a common and effective way of tackling the vital problem of rousing interest in and support for language work. The dangers and difficulties of this kind of event are fairly easy to predict. Outside speakers may well talk at a level which mystifies rather than enlightens, or skilful speakers may well arouse an initial enthusiasm that turns into frustration when the follow-up is lacking. A day conference cannot solve the organizational problems of putting the Bullock Report into practice. At School 1 the conference considered two proposals: the setting up of a number of working groups of staff from different subject areas to look into various aspects of 'language and learning' and 'the consideration on a departmental basis of proposals for developing concepts related to language and learning'. Even though the second proposal may sound intellectually more daunting than the first, it was the one that most staff opted for, because it tied language and learning to what could make sense for them – their own classroom teaching.

It was around the time of the conference launching the school's language policy work that the head was reconsidering the effect of hierarchy and authority in the school, and began to open director of faculty (faculties here were joint-subject departments) and head of house meetings to the rest of his staff. This was closely connected with the head's own views on language and learning: 'Language study and language development do not really flourish in a system or in an institution where you have strong authority feelings – it's the way we come at teachers and the way teachers come at kids that is very important in this.' These ideas were to be an important influence in the eventual development and degree of success of language across the curriculum at the school.

In the following few months, work seemed to go in two directions. A number of departments were getting involved in curriculum development of their own subject areas in which language and learning would eventually come to be considered. Immediately after the conference many teachers felt that they still had no way of appreciating what the language debate might imply for them, and could return to it only after the more immediate interests of curriculum change had been worked out. Meanwhile, on a more public level, regular meetings of general interest, on the theme of language and learning, were held – each attended by about a dozen staff. For example, after a discussion about pupils' activities during time spent in school, it was decided that two members of staff should each follow round a pupil for a day and report back on the pupil's language experiences. The results of this little investigation were reported back to a language meeting. However, the volunteer, come-if-you-wish nature of these fruitful meetings, although useful for the teachers present, did not ensure that the work and what could be learned from it would feed back directly into departments and enable a re-thinking of practices. It was not until later, when language and learning came to be seen as a central, school-wide issue that this problem of effective dissemination was overcome.

In another in this series of meetings the Head of English met the school's twelve probationary teachers and talked to them about language and learning, a perhaps obvious, but sometimes forgotten, bit of useful in-service work. What to do about your head of English is almost certain to be a problem for schools taking language and learning seriously. Many heads are quite rightly concerned about the prospect of a head of English apparently telling colleagues from other departments that he or she knows more about their teaching than they do themselves. School 1 possibly had more reason than most for being concerned. The head himself had been (and still remained) an English teacher, as was the deputy in charge of curriculum. The English department at the school was strong and vocal. It was particularly important that the department should play a very ordinary part in language across the curriculum and so, apart from this one meeting, the expertise of the Head of English was not officially called upon.

A later meeting of all staff took as its topic an issue that had hovered in the background in all the small, informal meetings: the relationship between language and discipline in school. It was partly this discussion that led the head to write a major policy statement on 'Relationships and discipline procedure', in which he argued that discipline is about relationships with children, not about the management and control of them. He was recognizing that there are connections between the language we use, the authority structures mediated in that language and the notion of discipleship implicit and explicit in that language. As he said to me: 'If you adopt an authoritarian stance in the classroom then the children are not going to develop language because the message you are giving them all the time is against this.' There was a recognition, too, that developing language is going to mean that work need not necessarily be silent (in fact a substantial part of my accounts of lessons shows work going on through talk). If a headteacher, or a head of department, feels that the only effective work is silent, solitary writing or reading (and many still do feel this), then the chances of effective language across the curriculum being developed in a school seem to be very limited.

In spite of the head's remarkable sensitivity to the widest implications of a language policy, not everything went right or smoothly and at times he felt very worried and disappointed. People were suspicious that perhaps Bullock was just the latest gimmick and possibly they felt, too, that it was being given prominence simply because it was the newly arrived deputy's way of making his mark on the school. School 1 seemed to be facing at that time a dilemma which I found in all the case study schools. It is this: unless there is leadership from the top, whatever is to be introduced and developed will have no status or influence in the school, yet, at the same time, if the innovation is seen to be imposed from above it may well be resisted because it has not developed out of ordinary teachers' needs. This is a dilemma which has to do with the special nature of language and learning. It is simply not usual for schools to take on a curriculum issue that is the concern of *every* department. Given that there are going to be demands on free time, and given that most people will have only the vaguest notion of possible benefits and outcomes, sustaining this work will need a committed effort. It is everyone's responsibility, yet it must be seen to rest with someone in particular.

The deputy head did in fact sustain his commitment during this stage – through the series of meetings which I have mentioned. Unfortunately they lacked a structure that would ensure the regular attendance of the same people, so that there was no guarantee that reports of meetings would be taken back into departments. Although language across the curriculum kept going and, as we have seen in the case of the policy statement on discipline, was being encouraged by the head as an issue of far-reaching importance, the essential links between studying language and classroom practice were not being forged.

Within a number of departments, nevertheless, progress was being made in taking language and learning into the classroom. For example, the History Department took up the Schools Council History 13–16 Project[1] and the Geography Department the Schools Council Geography 14–18 material.[2] Subject-centred curriculum development seems for many teachers to avoid some of the problems of language in learning. First of all, its speaks directly to one's concerns as a specialist teacher and does not imply that one has been doing things all wrong hitherto. Secondly, the kind of 'in-service' support given by the History Project (materials, meetings and discussions) takes some of the back-breaking work out of making new materials and some of the isolation out of working up new ideas.

The work undertaken by these departments had clear implications for language and learning. The shift in the conception of school history from the blank presentation of 'the story of the past' to using evidence and resources to piece that story together enabled the teachers to appreciate language at work in a way that they had not done before (see the 'Humanities revisited' section of this case study on pp. 69–70 below). Meanwhile, the History and Geography Departments were working together on a combined Humanities course for first and second years, another opportunity to reconsider syllabus and methodology from a sense of shared expertise.

At the same time the English Department was initiating important work related to language and learning. One of these initiatives resulted in the Enquiry course, which was seminal in the subsequent growth of language across the curriculum in the school (see the 'Enquiry revisited' section of this case study, pp. 71–75). Another was the Reading Development Programme (pp. 36–43). An interesting outcome of this curriculum development compared with the Humanities course was that it centred on language and learning, reflecting the greater confidence the English Department had in taking on language and learning in its own right. A further initiative by the department was a series of informal pub evenings, meetings open to all, usually with a topic introduced by an outside speaker, which were sometimes directly concerned with language. These meetings also give an indication of how very actively engaged with educational ideas the school was. Not all schools are.

School 1 was emerging as a place in which teachers from a number of departments took their own continuing education seriously, and devoted considerable time to it. The head recognized this. He saw, for instance, that history in the school was being transformed by 'in-service' work, and that language across the curriculum itself was about the continuing education of teachers. With the idea of being able to 'tie up ideas experimentally in our own classrooms', he approached his local education authority, asking them to make funds available for a place for one person in each of the authority's schools each year to do an Open University course: either Reading Development or Language and Learning. The cost would be £65 per taker. Money was short, the authority said, and turned down the request. The head was able to pay for his own Reading Development course, realizing as he did so that he was in a much more fortunate position than many young teachers with families to support.

FURTHER WORK

The story of the first phase of language across the curriculum in School 1 has shown language work coming up against numerous difficulties. Initial enthusiasm petered out; teachers retreated to their departments to work on the curriculum in terms they could understand; the small-group meetings on language, although stimulating and a continuing feature of school life, did not ensure links with departments. When I first visited the school, though, in May 1977 – eighteen months after the first tentative moves towards a language policy – it had become a different place, and one more amenable to the developments that were to characterize the second phase of language work. The policy about relationships and discipline, and certainly the airing that the whole matter had had, was resulting in an easing of relationships between staff and pupils in a school that the head and deputy felt had already been a friendly one. The curriculum deputy was now no longer new, and although much of the curriculum development which had taken place had been under the aegis of individual departments, the concern with language across the curriculum had been kept alive by him. Staff were now familiar with the idea and many of them were realizing that even though 'language across the curriculum' was a term that they could make little sense of, 'language and learning' was another matter. Some of them had seen, for instance in the case of the Humanities course, that one result of changing the syllabus was a change in the pattern of language activities. But perhaps most important of all, in the second phase of language activity on a school level, was the strategy of the deputy head. He approached each head of department to ask his or her department to choose a representative to be a member of a new Language and Learning Committee. He hoped to avoid the difficulty of language across the curriculum being just a come-if-you-please affair by arranging the appointment of someone with commitment to and responsibility for the work in each department.

The first meeting of the newly formed committee, which took place towards the end of my first visit to School 1, was particularly encouraging. The deputy head sensed a willingness on the part of members 'to accept that one does not know what is going on in others' lessons', and to admit that one has very little idea of what it feels like to be a pupil. (The outcome of this and subsequent meetings is reported in the 'Revisit' section of this case study.) This openness and commitment was encouraged by some important practical support from the head: it was possible, for example, for the minutes of the meeting to be typed and duplicated in the school office and sent out within two days. Facilities that can be taken for granted in almost every other profession are not always available to teachers. It matters that, when extra work is going to be asked of teachers, a little secretarial help of this kind should be available as a matter of course.

Aspects of English

An ambition which many English departments would claim for themselves, and one which this department was working at, is to enable children to feel that they have something valid to say, and to give them skilled guidance and thus the opportunity to become effective writers of stories or poems. One could see children in the English area in School 1 busily at work on stories or tapes and sense their feeling that English was 'a good subject' for which they had time and energy. The commitment of a strong teaching team, sharing ideas, had meant that the department had built up topics, and the resources for them, which provided a variety of class, group or individual work and which were designed to give a child the chance to take on an idea in his or her own way, which non-stop class teaching with everyone doing 'the same thing' cannot do. But equally important was the department's ability to develop teachers sensitive enough to listen and comment constructively – or often simply to let the child be. For instance the deputy head in charge of language across the curriculum had reached a stage in his relationship with his fourth-year class where he could see his pupils make an increasing commitment to their work. He and I looked through the folder of one boy and could see how for some time he had consistently written a side for each piece of work he had done and then, suddenly, he had written fifteen sides of a thoughtful, reflective diary. In talking with his teacher the boy had come to appreciate the flow of his own feeling within the repetitiveness of everyday routine. This had given him the confidence to write about his ordinary experiences. The encouragement which can lead to this kind of interest is not easy to document. Compared with some lessons, English may look unstructured – *laissez-faire*, even. But the teacher in this case had spent a lot of time re-thinking how he was using materials (stories, poems, pictures). He had become critical of his manipulation of material to make a 'successful lesson', rather than offering a child the material appropriate for him or her at a particular time. Many English teachers know how a child can move into new ways of feeling and understanding because they have been lucky enough, or aware enough, to offer the right poem or story at the right moment. Such occasions have little to do with the English teaching that gets children to turn arbitrary lists of adjectives into corresponding adverbs or, for example, 'write a sentence using correctly each of the following ten words'. The teaching done by this teacher did not involve pupils doing that kind of mechanical exercise (supposedly necessary to subsequent, more subtle language activities), but it required them to work with language to order and reflect on their own experiences – a process which probably will not fit conveniently into a lesson slot. Some of the best pieces of work done by this fourth-year class had come in from boys or girls who had written very little in actual lesson time, but had used that time to mull over ideas, selecting or dismissing, and had done the writing at home.

I intend this brief account of English at the school to highlight two aspects of its work which I see as critical. These are

    a that the child's view (and its expression) was taken seriously. The children in the school realized that it was, and responded by producing a lot of good, varied writing.

    b that the teacher was constantly reflecting upon and re-appraising his or her practices.

The Reading Development Programme and the Enquiry course which I describe in the following sections owe much of their success to the effective implementation of these principles by the teachers concerned.

The Reading Development Programme

The Reading Development Programme was established in the English Department, but was also greatly helped by the support of the headmaster, who chose to move a teacher to where she could most effectively modify the pattern of reading in the school. The teacher moved from working on the Humanities course and within the Remedial Department into the English Department, where she took on responsibility for a broad reading programme – a series of moves bound up with her increasing knowledge of the teaching of reading after taking the Open University's Reading Development course. Both the head and this teacher were encouraged to give reading an increased importance by contact with the Effective Use of Reading team from Nottingham University who used the school in their survey of reading.[3]

One part of the Reading Development Programme was called 'reading for pleasure'. Groups of children would come out of an English lesson to visit the reading room, which has bright curtains, floor cushions and a couple of tables – a heartening recognition that many children, like teachers, find classrooms uncongenial places in which to read. The teacher and an assistant, maybe a mother, would have her own 'client' children. Listening to children read, talking over their books with them, doing the difficult job of showing them how to browse and select a book they could get along with, were all part of the reading for pleasure work. There were several shelves of books in the reading room, but sometimes the teacher or helper would go to the school library with her 'clients' to give further guidance in browsing and choosing. In this work the teacher recognized that a child's not wanting to read and not getting along with books may have very little to do with how well he or she can read, and much more to do with not having been shown how to select wisely. This lack of guidance may also explain why many children return to the same author again and again. The teacher tried to find out, too, what reading the child did at home and how much encouragement he or she got. A lot of the children in the school come from affluent, spick-and-span homes which do not contain books.

The most successful and popular 'reads' in the reading room were short things that could be finished in a lesson. The Oxford University Press Storyhouse series was popular from this point of view, as was the school's Storyshelf, a shelf of books of stories, poems and articles written by children in the school and written out, but more usually typed, and put in a folder. The Storyshelf represented a lot of hard work by members of the English Department. In the reading for pleasure sessions a child might very well come with his or her own written work which he or she and teacher could read together. These were also the sessions when the teacher could check technical things such as full stops or spelling mistakes. But, significantly, reading for pleasure was not regarded by the teacher in charge, or by the English Department who released children, as a remedial operation. Children of all kinds of needs, ages and stages came to the sessions.

The reading teacher felt that it was important to get to know the children at work away from the reading room and she would spend a number of lessons each week in English classes where she might share the teaching of a drama lesson, or work with a group of children as they wrote their stories. She would also mark books with a teacher. Her work was not organized or treated as a stop-gap in the department, but was genuinely co-operative.

The decision to give this teacher an overall responsibility for reading in the school and enable her to work co-operatively with the English Department had been taken because this was how it was felt reading development could most readily flourish. Before the move to establish the Reading Development Programme, the English Department had been reviewing its practices on reading. In the early days of language across the curriculum discussion in the school they had begun to feel that they should look more closely at reading levels. 'Perhaps we were not looking at the books we were giving them as closely as possible,' and perhaps, although giving encouragement to children, 'we were not aiming at anything in particular'. I quote these two remarks from a member of the English Department. She and the department were far from smug about what they were achieving. They were not saying things like the dismissive 'we already do that', and they had no intuitive certainty that they were on the right lines. This teacher, while still in her probationary year, visited a number of schools in the area which along with School 1 had had joint language policy meetings, organized by H M Is and local advisers, shortly after the publication of *A Language for Life*. She was interested in reading development in those schools and was glad to find that one outcome of these meetings was to provide informal contacts which enabled visits such as this. The reading work she found in one of the schools was 'too narrow in terms of English' with no work on stories and poems and an overriding concern with reading 'to gather information'. One school, however, was using a technique which this teacher had heard of but had not seen in action: group prediction. She began to find material of the kind she felt was appropriate for her department and she introduced group prediction and group sequencing. A brief explanation of these two activities may be helpful.

Group prediction

    a A story (or extract) is divided up. (In this case it was typed and cut into sections. Each section was mounted on card and covered with library film. Several copies were made.)

    b Each child (in groups of about six or eight) is given the first section to read silently.

    c With the guidance of a leader (usually a teacher, possibly a sixth-former or helper) the group discusses what has happened in the first section, and tries to predict what will happen.

    d Section 1 is collected in, Section 2 is given out. Everyone reads it silently and then, in discussion, he or she is able to check the accuracy of the group's predictions and to predict further.

    e The reading and predicting continues until the story comes to an end.

Group sequencing

    a A story or poem is divided up as in **a** above.

    b All the cards for the story or poem are jumbled up and given out all at once. The group, in pairs, works out a possible order for the story.

    c The pairs come together to compare and justify their sequences.

    d They may or may not then compare their versions with the author's. (The stress is on achieving a plausible sequence rather than the correct one.)

The department found that, with poems or stories, prediction was a more fruitful exercise than sequencing, that it offered more to work on, and so used prediction more often. Both exercises were seen in this school as very useful with mixed-ability groups, because all pupils had the opportunity to reflect on their reading. Reading was deliberately done alone at first so that if some children had misread, 'by talk and questioning later they can re-read and organize their ideas without seeming to be wrong'. Virtual non-readers were not included in the groups, as the interpretive and checking work requires pupils to be able to see – on close, careful inspection – what the text 'actually says'. At first the department experimented with a scheme whereby on a particular day in the week a class would be divided into three groups, one of which would do prediction, another sequencing, the third reading for pleasure. The following week each group would change to a new activity, and a new one again in the week after that. The work later broadened out to include 'reading extensions' which could involve re-creating stories in groups, often with the help of a tape-recorder. As the reader will have gathered, this class's reading development schedule for a half term involved some fairly complex organization.

I was interested to learn what effect group reading development work had on 'ordinary' English lessons. One teacher explained that she and others in the department were able to use the children's familiarity with group activities. For instance, in talking about introductions to their stories, the question 'How can you make it so that I want to read on?' could lead a class to discuss a particularly successful opening to a prediction story. A number of children in a third-year class said explicitly to this teacher that prediction had made them more aware of openings and endings and variety in their own story-writing. I quote below an extract from a group prediction session – a relatively long transcript, although it represents only a few minutes from one forty-minute tape. It indicates something of the range of discussion that took place, and illustrates the role of the group leader (in this case the deputy head). The way the teacher gives leads without telling answers, and takes up, refers back to and works on the basis of what pupils have said, is a fine example of giving children control over their own language and learning. The extract should also give those many people unfamiliar with prediction an idea of the activity's distinctive flavour.

The group of seven had come along to the deputy head's room, found themselves chairs and settled down, joking about the tape-recorder; they were then given the first card. The transcript begins after the group has read the second section.

Invitation to a Ghost

1 Ivan and Alexei had grown up together in the same village in Russia. They had played together as small children, gone to school together, and when they became young men they always went together to the besydas, the evening gatherings where young people met to talk and sing and dance.

The two friends were also good-natured rivals. Sometimes Ivan would be the first to do a thing; at other times Alexei would score over his friend, but in the long run they were evenly matched in their accomplishments.

2 One day Ivan and Alexei were talking about their future, and the subject of marriage was naturally mentioned. They knew that they would not be able to see as much of each other when each of them had a wife to keep, but they made a solemn pact that whichever married first would invite the other to the wedding. Then followed more friendly rivalry. Who would be the bride-groom and who would be the wedding guest?

'If I marry first,' said Ivan, 'I'll invite you to the wedding whether you're alive or dead!'

'That goes for me too,' said Alexei solemnly.

*

Some months passed, during which the young men worked and played together, and then Alexei was suddenly stricken by a mysterious disease, and died after several weeks of illness. Ivan was very sad at losing his friend, and for a time felt lost and lonely. He recovered his high spirits, however, when he fell in love with one of the village girls, and when she agreed to marry him he was overjoyed.

TEACHER There's an awful lot packed in there, isn't there? In this second sec-
tion – an awful lot happens – why are you all gasping?
VOICE It's that part, he'll invite him alive or dead, and he died.
TEACHER So you think that's an important bit of it?
ANOTHER VOICE Yes, well he'll come back, won't he, when he gets married, whatsisname will come back. He says he'll invite him whether he's alive or dead.
JULIE That's silly, 'whether you're alive or dead'. How can you invite a dead person?
VOICES [much of it inaudible] Yes, but . . .
BOY Soon grown up, haven't they?
TEACHER Yes, the story's moved on very quickly, as you say. What did you say, Julie, about alive or dead?
JULIE 'Alive or dead'. That's a horrible statement to make. You don't tell people, 'If you're dead I'll still invite you.' You don't talk about dying when you're only that age.
TEACHER Do you think it's a funny thing to have said?
JULIE I think it's very strange.

TEACHER Does that give you some clue, I mean is that why you think it's important . . . for the future of the story, because it's such an unusual thing to say?

JULIE Well I mean it seems funny that he said, 'if you're alive or dead', and then a few minutes later he died.

VOICE (GIRL) Oh no, it says some months passed.

TEACHER Months, yes.

VOICE It didn't show you how his friendship –

JULIE Yes, but do you say to someone, 'Alive or dead you're coming to my wedding'? I wouldn't, anyway.

CAROL But then you made it sound like an order. He just said, 'If I marry first I invite you to the wedding, whether you're alive or dead.' I mean, it doesn't mean he's going to come.

VOICE It's intention.

JULIE [in a ghostly voice] Alex, I know you're there.

TEACHER Well, he has died, hasn't he? One of them has died, Alexie has died.

CAROL A mysterious disease.

TEACHER Do you think the mysterious disease is significant?

CAROL Or they could have put an unknown disease or german measles or flu or something. But they put a mysterious disease.

BOY And then he's married a bit later on.

TEACHER Then the other one, Ivan, gets married, right.

VOICE (GIRL) They haven't married yet, though they've agreed to marry. Something could happen, he could come back and get scared or something.

JULIE He hasn't had much of a life. He fell in love with a girl and then he's marrying her.

TEACHER What do you mean, he hasn't had much of a life?

VOICE Well, one girl and that's it.

TEACHER You don't know if that's the only one.

CAROL In Russia that's how they are.

VOICE How do you know?

TEACHER Well, doing all this stamping and flag-waving, they haven't got much time left [a reference to an earlier remark by one of them that she associated Russia with stamping and flag-waving].

CAROL No, I mean [laughing], oh anyway, it doesn't matter.

TEACHER Yes, go on.

CAROL It just seems a bit strange. It says he met a girl and fell in love with her and that's the end. And one of his village girls. He hadn't even gone round and had a look around.

VOICE Usually that would be for an ending of a story, they get married and lived happily ever after.

VOICE Yes, very quick ending.

TEACHER Well, perhaps this is the end. Is this the end?

VOICE No, there are ten more to go.

TEACHER Oh, I told you. If this were the end do you think it would have been a very satisfactory story?

LOTS OF VOICES No – very quick.

TEACHER Very quick, yes, but would it have been perhaps fleshed out more, if this had been all it had been about?

MUDDLE OF VOICES Yes, but that's left that sentence, 'If I am married first I invite you to my wedding alive or dead,' that's left that sentence.

[*After a few seconds the teacher picks up one remark.*]

TEACHER Carol, you said something about what might be about to happen, because you said he isn't married.

CAROL Well, they've agreed to marry. They haven't married yet. Something could easily happen – she could die or he could.

VOICE Maybe he's talked about marrying and then he's scared to marry.

VOICE It seems so quick.

VOICE Maybe there's got to be a complication.

VOICE Yes, maybe – like Carol says – Alexie or whatever his name is comes back and kills Ivan's wife.

VOICE [*laughter*] He's doing it again.

TEACHER He's looking ahead, though. Can we have the next part. What do you think is going to happen?

VOICE They'll get married.

TEACHER They will get married, do you think?

VOICE They'll have a big wedding, I should think, and something will happen at the wedding.

VOICES The reception . . . Alexie or something . . . he'll come . . . because alive or dead . . . he'll come . . . he'll come as a ghost.

TEACHER Will he?

VOICE Yes.

TEACHER But the bit in this section does mention an actual invitation, doesn't it? After he's dead how's he going to invite him?

VOICE But it's a thing he said. So he'll remember it, won't he?

VOICE [*in a ghostly style*] I know you're there, come out.

TEACHER Is there going to be some definite invitation, or are the words that he said to his friend, 'dead or alive', enough?

VOICE He didn't say, 'You're invited to the wedding.' He said, 'You'll be invited to the wedding.'

TEACHER So he hasn't invited him.

VOICE So he's got to invite him. If he'd said, 'You're invited to the wedding whether you're alive or dead,' well, then he was invited, but 'I will invite you' means that he's yet to invite.

VOICE Maybe, maybe.

VOICE It says they made a solemn promise that whoever got married first would come to the wedding.

VOICE But you don't remember statements . . . if you're . . . if I said you wouldn't remember . . . the ghost is going to come and say, 'You invited me to the wedding.'

BOY Maybe, I think maybe Ivan forgets to invite him and that he comes back or something.

TEACHER Oh yes, he's broken his promise.

VOICE Yes, he's broken his promise.

VOICE Yes, I think he'll forget that he's said that.

VOICE He'll be so overjoyed about getting married, he won't remember.

BOY Because it was a long time ago. Yes, that's the thing. That was when they were still children, they said that, but then some months passed and they're young men.

TEACHER Yes, so there was a period of growing up.

BOY So he could forget that, couldn't he?

TEACHER OK. Should we go on, then?

Sometimes when prediction is described to teachers the reply comes back: 'Oh, we do that already, we do that when we read a textbook together, it's part of our normal reading.' As I hope that this extract shows, group prediction is something quite different from reading a book in class and talking about it. It has a game-like quality about it, an excitement and a concentration that are unmistakable as one is present or as one listens to a tape and which are perhaps not altogether lost in the transcript. The discussion shows how very detailed the pupils' reading of the text is and illustrates the way in which the members of the group return to the text for evidence for their arguments, with an impressive, subtle and developing appreciation of the nuances of the story. There are interruptions in the transcript, as there are in any conversation, but the members are listening to each other, taking up each other's points. The extracts also show how the member identified as 'BOY' gradually takes a more full part in the discussion. This boy was physically much smaller than the two dominant members of the group, the girls Carol and Julie, and had a much more childish voice. Not only does he successfully muscle in, but he picks up and puzzles over detail from the extract to argue his point about the broken promise. No doubt the reader will be able to draw further inferences or form more detailed impressions about the logic and structure of the discussion – particularly if he or she has previously used and studied tapes of conversation.

The Reading Development Programme was not simply going to be repeated in the following years. It was subject to scrutiny and reshaping, as it had already been in the decision to favour prediction more than sequencing. The strength of the programme was that, by making public aspects of reading which are usually private – puzzling one's way round a library and selecting or rejecting a book; making meaning from a text, etc. – it was enabling the English Department to have a much fuller understanding of what happens to children when they read.

Enquiry

At the time of my first visit to School 1 plans were going ahead to extend a joint English/Science experimental venture called 'Enquiry', the idea for which had initially arisen from the English Department's worries about the whole complex of relationships which are usually sustained in teaching/learning situations where teachers act as the enlightened, children as would-be initiates into knowledge. One member of the department went ahead with the thinking and working out of ideas. From talks with members of the Science Department this teacher had realized that English and science teachers of first years had in fact a common aim: they both, albeit for different reasons, wanted children to use their senses to observe closely. The concern of the scientist would be to encourage the systematic observation of phenomena critical for the development of scientific method, and the English Department's concern would be with the child's using his or her senses freshly and being true to those experiences in his or her use of language. After a more formal meeting about the possibility of the two departments working together, the English teacher produced a duplicated booklet containing pieces of writing which exemplified looking closely. Some pieces were by children in the school, others by professional writers. Many of the pieces, which are to do with observing plant life or wildlife, link the concerns of English and science teachers. The booklet was prefaced by an important passage from the Bullock Report:

It is a confusion of everyday thought that we tend to regard 'knowledge' as something that exists independently of someone who knows. 'What is known' must in fact be brought to life afresh in every 'knower' by his own efforts . . . In order to accept what is offered when we are told something, we have to have somewhere to put it; and having somewhere to put it means that the framework of past knowledge and experience into which it must fit is adequate as a means of interpreting and apprehending it. Something approximating to 'finding out for ourselves' needs therefore to take place if we are to be successfully told.[4]

By talking about knowledge and knowing, the passage adopts a vocabulary familiar to teachers of subjects which can be seen much more readily than English as bodies of knowledge. But its argument shifts the emphasis from 'the body' of knowledge and, by treating knowledge as the processes of coming to know, points to the possible links between knowing and using languages.

As there seemed to be a plausible basis for a coherent first-year course, the English and Science Departments agreed to work together on a project that would involve about four pairs of teachers (one from each department) taking groups, which would normally have had one separate lesson in each subject, together for two lessons. The first job for these pairs of teachers was to secure some independence from the two departments, since Enquiry was not to be about teaching English or science but about developing ideas of how children may be encouraged to direct their own learning without the usual stipulations about 'covering the ground' or 'doing it in order'. The work would be experimental for teachers and for pupils, with the teacher not able simply to rely on his or her own expertise in the 'content' of a subject but having also to attend to the way in which pupils' learning was organized. The drama workshop, some lockable cupboards and a small budget were allocated to the project and one of the participating teachers prepared the following guidelines as to how the work might be approached, to keep the head and other colleagues informed of progress:

'Enquiry' – Science/English link-up

A. SOME POSSIBLE STARTING POINTS
1. *'Communication'* – animal signalling system; human verbal/non-verbal communication, para-language through gestures, facial expression, tone, etc.; the artificial media, print, photos, TV – 'Sounds' – noise – talk – music.
2. *'Natural life study'* – birds, animals, insects, fish – type, behaviour and habitat.
3. *'Natural habitat study'* – trees, plants, fungi, ponds, possible extension into ecology/conservation.
4. *'Safety'* – via fire, flood, chemical and electrical hazards – in the countryside, on the roads, in the home, at school, etc.
5. *'Food'* – natural and artificial foodstuffs, cultivation, culinary construction [?], manufacture – taste, texture, diet and digestion.
6. *'Transport'* – muscular and mechanical, natural and artificial – 'flight' – again natural and man-made forms.
7. *'My body'* – What makes me work? Why am I like I am?
8. *'Memory'* – Techniques and tricks, selectivity, dreams, etc.
9. *'My village'* – ecology, social economy, biography, etc.

B. SOME POSSIBLE WORKING GROUPS
(Core teams plus students, mums, sixth-formers, etc.)
[There follows a list of pairs of teachers to work together, doubling up classes.]

C. SOME POSSIBLE WORKING AREAS
Combination of drama workshop and library – therefore need for constant consultation with librarian.

D. SOME POSSIBLE PROBLEMS
Finance! – need for basic stock of exercise books, folders, paper (and display paper), scissors, glue, Sellotape, etc. Basic reprographic requirement (therefore need for consultation with resources officer) plus modest stock of books – perhaps a selection of materials from the Penguin Primary Projects on 'Food', 'Communications', 'My Body', etc. Any other?

These 'possible starting points' for Enquiry may look simply arbitrary in terms of a conventional syllabus. They were used by the Enquiry team to suggest to children what they could choose to examine if they themselves didn't have the confidence to put up their own ideas. The emphasis was very clearly on the techniques rather than the object of observation, as the statement of aims and observations reproduced here as Figure 1 shows. These notes were produced by the teacher who had developed the original Enquiry idea and who was to become acknowledged as the *de facto* leader of the team of Enquiry teachers.

Enquiry

General aim
To encourage independent, active learners with 'enquiry' minds (in this sense the approach or learning process to take precedence over 'end products', 'content' or 'results')

through

closely observing, exploring and ordering observations (to include various technical skills concerned with library work, etc.)

through

oral expression   *visual & pictorial expression*

written expression
Starting point to be an honest or accurate account of observations or findings:
'Looking closely'

to include thinking aloud in print – posing possibilities, questions, new lines of development:
'Expressive writing'

leading towards

subjective meaning for oneself: *explicit* meaning for others:
'poetic writing'   *'expository or factual writing'*

Figure 1 Aims of School 1's Enquiry course

The outcome of the Enquiry work initiated in September 1977 and its influence on the language across the curriculum movement in the school is considered in the 'Revisit' section of this study. I turn now to mention the Enquiry pilot exercise which was under way on my first visit to the school (in summer 1977) and which led into the later work. This first Enquiry course was run for just two classes for one afternoon per week. An English teacher (the head of department) and an art teacher were time-tabled for the session, but as many other helpers as possible were recruited. The headmaster worked with some of the group, as did a lecturer from the nearby university, and I too (literally, as it happened) mucked in.

By the time I joined the Enquiry project, at the beginning of the summer term, most of the children had moved on from keeping journals about 'looking closely', the best containing deceptively simple accounts, anecdotes and reports (for example, of growing shoots from seeds – a holiday activity suggested by the teacher). At this stage any number of activities could make an Enquiry afternoon. For instance, one group regularly visited a nearby brook to observe some of the life and changes in it; another group, which I joined, was visiting the local churchyard to clean up some of the graves and talk with the vicar about the church. They eventually became interested in the number of graves of very young children. It was at this stage, too, that the Head of English was able to see the dangers in this kind of work. For a number of children it was becoming little more than time-filling busywork. But there had been enough good work to be encouraging: carefully kept journals, small experiments carefully documented, with the children showing a sensitivity in observing, recording, asking, and setting out their work – whether for display or for their friends, teachers and parents to read. The example which follows shows a fine balance of observation and speculation.

The Snowdrop

If you look at a snowdrop in detail you can see some very interesting things.

The head of the flower is not all white, if you look closely at the inner petals on the inside there is some green, it is not just plain green, it is in stripes.

Two centimetres down from the head there is a little translucent pouch. When the flower is still in the form of a bud the pouch protects it from the cold weather. When it is warm enough

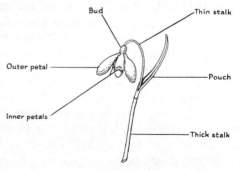

the pouch will move back, letting the flower open up. If you try to put the flower back into the pouch you will find that the thin stalk gets in the way.

If the pouch and the stalk both grow at the same pace the bud would never get out of the pouch so the bud would never get out without growing quicker than the pouch or the pouch growing slower than the bud. That could be why the stalk is thinner near the top.

LOOKING CLOSELY

Snowdrop ...
It's fragile, dainty. The flower is triangular-shaped, heart-shaped. If you squeeze the petals together it looks like a trumpet. When it's open it's the shape of a propeller or hair-dryer. The white bit is like a hat. Looked at another way, the outside pattern is like a donkey's ears. The white petals have what looks like veins painted on them. The middle bits are like arrows.

An old snowdrop was droopy and looked like a cauliflower; but a new snowdrop looks like a fairy on a string or like a fairy lantern with the middle bits like fairy candles.

If you put the stem in your mouth it tastes like honey-water – honey-water from sugar flowers. The stem and the flower are smooth everywhere but the stem is slippery and the middle parts feel furry.

You can open up the part where the flower has come from, and if you do you will find it partially transparent.

Mathematics

The Head of Mathematics was very articulate about the links between language, learning and his own subject. He had developed an approach to his subject which, in his eyes, entailed certain ways of working and placed special emphasis on language, particularly upon small-group talk. An important distinction he made about mathematics in schools was between 'teacher tell' teaching ('I'll show you how to do this. This is how you do it. Please go away and do ten more.') and the kind of teaching concerned with enabling a child to see and take on a problem. The first kind of teaching, he felt, had resulted in the plight of some of the first-years coming into the school who had been taught a rule for multiplication, say, but were puzzled when their rule broke down, and probably had no understanding of how and why the number resulting from multiplication was bigger than the two numbers multiplied. In the case of such children, who need to establish basic techniques that will give them greater power in their subsequent work in mathematics, this teacher tried to present a technique in a context offering the child some freedom to arrive at his or her own understanding. How this may look in practice is illustrated by the first extract – from a lesson on multiplication – reproduced below.

Since in the first and second years mathematics is taught in mixed-ability groups and children coming into the school will have had a variety of mathematical experience, and because textbooks are often unsuitable for such a diverse group, there is considerable reliance on worksheets. The head of department appreciated the difficulties that worksheets may present and felt anxious that they should offer freedom for the child to work at something from his or her own initiative. Therefore he built into them a variety of activities so that children don't just operate a worksheet formula. For instance, children were sent to do some work in the school grounds or area round the school (for 'distance measuring') or to the mathematics prep room to work with scales.

Just as this teacher had distinguished in teaching style between 'teacher telling' and posing problems, he distinguished, in mathematics, between techniques and processes. Essentially, he said, mathematics is about processes and learning about processes involves a willingness to see or to take on a mathematical problem. He gave me an example of what he meant: 'If I put three coins on a table facing up tails and say to you, "I'm going to turn them over two at a time," so I turn them over and two of them are heads and one of them is tails and I keep on doing that and I say to you, "Will you get them all heads for me?", a real mathematics problem-taker would work through that problem and then probably change the rules, would put down four coins perhaps, and then change the rules for turning them over (three at a time rather than two).' Each specific task set thus becomes an occasion to experiment and generalize about sequences, numbers of stages, rules of procedure and inference or whatever. This would be the first step in involving oneself in mathematical processes; the second step would be communicating what one has done, and finding a language for it. The language will enable one to lay out results, communicate rules, conjectures, speculations, give arguments for why certain results are true or false. Techniques begin to matter not so much for their own sake but because they give the pupil-mathematician more power to take up and work more deeply on a problem. It is here that one can appreciate why this teacher believed that even techniques should not just be taught as: 'I do this, you copy.' Pupils have to be able to see the relevance of a technique to a problem in hand and can only be successful if they understand the technique rather than if they simply know how to perform it.

I asked the head of department to say more about his view that finding and making a language to express the mathematics you have done is a critical stage in appreciating the nature of mathematics. He pointed out that number algebra, for instance, is a highly refined code, developed over centuries. He went on: 'If children are to be successful at accepting a code, a code developed by other people, then they have to go through a stage, not necessarily copying what happened historically, but probably approximately the same. There must be opportunity for them to write their own shorthand because mathematics relies on a tremendous amount of shorthand.' They must learn, too, he pointed out, to express numbers in symbolic form. Probably the children will start expressing symbolically everything that they already know; for instance they may devise symbols for $7 + 3 = 10$. In one part of School 1's first-year maths course pupils have the job of describing in shorthand the movement of shapes in frames. Devising such a shorthand convention, being able to understand the way it represents the movements and being able to make use of it gives them an approach to the abstractions of mathematics quite different from the one encouraged in a mathematics textbook classic whose opening statement to secondary school pupils is the cryptic and mystifying 'Let x be the unknown number.' An important principle is involved here. Pupils in these lessons are being given the opportunity to bring what they already know – something of the nature of mathematical codes – to what they are coming to know.

What these principles, teaching processes rather than techniques by starting from mathematical insights and moving to notation, look like in practice will – I hope – emerge from the following descriptions of classwork. All the maths lessons I report on here were with a mixed-ability first year, working in small groups that had been selected by the teacher, who placed pupils of similar mathematical attainment together. There were three main kinds of work: mathematical techniques such as multiplication and division; measurement of lengths, distances and weights; and work on number bases. The teacher was very conscientious about getting round to groups. At the end of each lesson he would know exactly whom he had seen and whom he had missed. He was also concerned about interviewing at the right time and using his conversations with groups not to tell them answers, but to ease them through a difficulty or extend a problem. He had had the opportunity to see a video-tape of himself at work, and he had been struck by how much in a lesson he had missed (even on the basis of the video's very partial picture of the lesson). He admitted that 'I have in some respects less knowledge of what's going on because there's more going on,' which seems, at least, better than knowing relatively more because there is less to know.

In the first lesson I recorded, two girls were at work on decimals. They had already finished a multiplication worksheet which suggested they use a table like this:

Thousands Hundreds Tens Units · tenths hundredths thousandths

which they now used to divide 46 by 10.

PUPIL 2 What does it mean, 'Divide by 10'?
PUPIL 1 Move back ten places – move back two places.
PUPIL 2 No, it says by 10, not 100.
PUPIL 1 By 10, that means move back to there.
PUPIL 2 Yes, but you don't do it two places, do you?
PUPIL 1 That goes to six.
PUPIL 2 Oh!
PUPIL 1 That's it, that goes there, that goes there and that goes there.
PUPIL 2 Oh, so you move all of them back one, instead of moving them forward.
PUPIL 1 Yes.
PUPIL 2 So the four goes there: instead of the four being under the ten you put it under the units, instead of the six being under the units you put it under the ten. instead of the ten . . .

The girls were doing what their teacher had hoped they would be doing at this stage of their work. They were moving towards a sense of what multiplication is by talking aloud over a diagram that helped them to see it. They were not simply manipulating hieroglyphics in mindless mastery of a skill: they were coming to understand a process. It was at this stage that the teacher, with a fine sense of timing, arrived on the scene:

TEACHER Can you explain why you do the opposite to multiply?
PUPIL 1 Why do you do the opposite, Paula?
PUPIL 2 I don't know.
PUPIL 1 When you're dividing you're going back.
TEACHER When you go forwards you're multiplying by ten and you're making the number bigger.
PUPIL 1 Yes.
TEACHER When you divide by ten what happens to the number?
PUPIL 2 You make it smaller.
TEACHER Make it smaller, and that's why you're shunting backwards.
PUPIL 2 But if you divide it by a hundred then you move it two.

It was a useful intervention, helping the girls to secure their understanding. The teacher suggested the connection between multiplication and division: they are opposite, inverse processes. But the girls couldn't go on from there and explain that multiplication makes numbers bigger, division makes them smaller. However, Pupil 1's comment, 'When you're dividing you're going back,' was enough for the teacher to pick up and point out the meaning of her statement with, 'When you go forwards you're multiplying by ten and you're making the number bigger.' Pupil 2, at least, was then able to take up what this implies for division.

The second group I looked at, in the same first-year mixed-ability class, had already covered the work that the first group were doing. They were now studying the measurement of length, weight and distance by means of the worksheet reproduced on p. 53. The pupils were not simply being asked to practise using a distance table, which, it could be argued, would be a very useful thing for them to do, but, in the questions in section 2, were being invited to consider different conventions for measuring distance, and different levels of accuracy for different purposes.

The question: 'Why is Manchester about 100 km from Nottingham?', was a great puzzle to two pupils.

PUPIL A Why is Manchester about 100 kilometres from Nottingham?
PUPIL B Why is it, or how?
PUPIL A Why is it?
   [*The tape-recorder was accidentally shifted and picked up a blur of noise for a few minutes. Then it picked up.*]
PUPIL A 'Why is Manchester about 100 kilometres from Nottingham?' Pippa, you know how it says 114 kilometres; could it be that they didn't measure it from the centre of Manchester and I have?
PUPIL B What?
   [*Pupil A managed to turn her friend's attention to the question and suggested again her reason for the different answers. Pupil B had her own ironic suggestion: 'Why? Because it was built there.'*]

Three days later, at the beginning of the class's next mathematics lesson, I went up to this group to be greeted by Pupil A with: 'Have you any idea why Nottingham is 100 kilometres from Manchester?' Her speculations had widened now: 'Would it be because when they first started it, because on here it's 100 miles as the crow flies and not going as the road goes, it's probably more going by the road.' I suggested that they called over their teacher, who, after asking the girls to look at the distance on the map (which gave a rough reading of 100 kilometres), turned their attention to the table:

TEACHER Now what type of table is that? What's it for? What kind of book would it come out of?
PUPIL A Er, maps. It's road distances.
TEACHER Road distances. Does that explain the difference between the 100 and 114?
PUPIL A As the crow flies it's 100 and by our roads it's more.
PUPIL B It says that one's 100 and that one's 114. It's where they measure it from. But we still don't know why it's 100 kilometres from the other one.

Distances over England, Wales and Scotland

For this you will need (a) a distance table
                      (b) map number 2.
You can write on the map.

1. After copying the following pairs of towns into your book, use the table to work out the distance between each pair. Underline each pair on the map.

Towns	Distance between them in km
London and Inverness Nottingham and Edinburgh Shrewsbury and Holyhead Plymouth and Hull Norwich and Bristol	

2. Using the scale at the bottom of your map open your compasses to a radius representing 100 km. Draw a circle with Nottingham as centre. Why is Manchester about 100 km from Nottingham? The table says 114 km. Why are the two answers different?

Repeat circles from '50 km radius' up to 350 km, all with Nottingham as centre.

Copy and complete the following table into your book:

Town	Distance from Nottingham in a straight line	Distance from Nottingham as given in the table
Buxton Lincoln Shrewsbury Northampton Hull Leeds York Blackpool Norwich Oxford London Bristol Edinburgh Darlington Dover		

PUPIL A It doesn't make sense.
TEACHER How do you mean, the question doesn't make sense?
PUPIL B Well, we've done it, why the differences are 114 and 100, but we still don't know why they are that fourteen apart from each other.

The girls were saying here that, although they had been able to appreciate that two kinds of measuring (straight line and road) would give two results, this did not seem satisfactorily to answer the question: 'Why is Manchester 100 km from Nottingham?' Misunderstandings such as this are a problem of even the most carefully made worksheets. You can't ask a worksheet what it really means: you can't get it to rephrase itself. The wording here, as interpreted by these two pupils (and this did not feature as a problem for others) was getting in the way of their understanding, so that even though they had worked out an answer to the problem, they did not realize they had done so because they felt that the question was asking for something else. Perhaps more important than the problem, though, was the fact that it came to light because the lesson was organized for the talking through of problems. The lesson seems to vindicate their teacher's belief that giving children problems within a framework, and giving them variety, will encourage them to work persistently.

Two boys in this first-year class were working on number bases and I was able to follow them taking on a problem, working it out in talk and making what they had done communicable to others. The boys, Robert and Neil, listened to a tape of a shepherd checking his sheep by counting: Yan, tyan, tethera, methera, pimp, sethera, lethera, havera, dovera, dick, yanadick, tyanadick, tetheradick, metheradick, bumfit, yanabumfit, tyanabumfit, tetherabumfit, metherabumfit, yiggit. They and their teacher then had a brief talk. Were there any rhythms, their teacher asked. Neil pointed out: 'They use the same end of the word, say, five times – using different beginnings.' The teacher, after talking about the periodic, continuous nature of counting systems – contrasted with 'counting out' rhymes, which always come to an end after a fixed number – then invited the boys to have a go at making their own counting system. They looked fairly briefly at the shepherd's count, reproduced in a booklet of work on number bases (produced by the Mathematics Department), and began work on their own. Robert started off, 'If you think about how the numbers go, they go one, two, three, four, five, six, seven, eight, nine, and then one nought, ten; one two, that's twelve; one three – like that. So if we start off by having, how many. Six words. Think of six words.' After a couple of dummy runs making long crazy lists of words, Neil picked up the dominant rhyme 'in' and said: 'OK, let me have a go, start with "ins". We'll start in fives and we'll go one, two, three, four, five – change the end of the word. One, two three, four, five – change the end of the word. OK?' In what seemed like no time at all, to my mathematically addled brain, they had produced: yin, sin, fin, pin, min. Having got that group of five, Neil then suggested that they wanted another group of five. But Robert came in with: 'No. That's five now, so you start off with yin-sin, yin-fin, yin-pin, yin-min.' Neil didn't understand:

NEIL What are you doing?
ROBERT That's how you do it. That's the next one, so that's yin, sin, fin, pin, min, yin-sin, yin-fin, yin-pin.
NEIL But you're using the same ones.
ROBERT Yes, I know. So that you only have to learn five number systems – five words and then you start off, starting off from yin-sin, yin-fin, yin-pin, yin-min – like that.

I was impressed with the pupils' willingness to get involved in a problem and see it through, an important step in this being a willingness to say when they didn't understand. This, I am sure, had something to do with relationships between the children, but it also had a great deal to do with the organization and running of lessons. The kinds of worksheets and materials supplied meant that pupils were adequately briefed and had resources to get on with their work. The teacher was then free to search out the children who needed help or who would profit from a conversation. In this case the teacher came in just as the two boys had written down: 'fin-yin, fin-sin, fin-fin, fin-min'. They told him their counting system. His question, 'I should think there are some interesting properties with numbers like yin-yin, sin-sin, fin-fin, pin-pin, min-min. What are they in our counting system?', very adroitly led the boys to a knot in their work. Could they articulate what they had done in order to tell someone else, and in order, perhaps, to see if they had been successful? At first they stumbled into answers: 'Ten, twenty, thirty, no – twenty-two, thirty-three,' until the teacher reminded them that they had been counting on a base-five system and asked them what was yin-yin in the conventional base-ten counting system. After one false start the penny audibly dropped and they chorused: 'Oh, six.' They worked out then that sin-sin was twelve (one false go to get that); fin-fin, Neil claimed, was eighteen. 'Was that a guess or a projection?' asked the teacher. 'A projection,' answered Neil. It sounded honest.

Not only had the teacher got the boys to do that difficult job of giving equivalents for their number so that the structure of their system was clear, he'd led them and himself to see a flaw:

TEACHER You've got, in fact, a base-six system because if you've got one, two, three, four and five you've also got nought as well. Perhaps – I don't know – unless you count yin as nought.
ROBERT Oh, we forgot that, didn't we?

The teacher and Robert puzzled over the paper on which Robert had written his numbers. They worked out together that if they used 'in' as nought, 'yin-in' and 'sin-in' would be in the counting series.

TEACHER Then yin-in would be your ...
ROBERT and NEIL Ten.
TEACHER Ten.
ROBERT and NEIL Sin-in, twenty.
NEIL Fin-in, thirty.
ROBERT So that you'd get sin-in-sin, something like that.
TEACHER What happens when you run out of all the twos? What does a three-digit number sound like in this system?
ROBERT Then you just start ... you have to think up another list, don't you? Something like –
NEIL If you had a lot of sheep you'd need more but we've only got fifty sheep.

Neil's joke marked the beginning of a very difficult time. Robert was puzzled about comparisons between their new number system and the ordinary number system. Remembering the ordinary number system was getting in the way. Although with either system you could count any number of things, because the two systems had different bases, numbers written in the same way – but in different systems – were not straightforwardly equivalent and could not stand for the same number of objects. For a time they lost what they had already established. Neil declared 'yin-yin' was ten. Robert put down 'yin-in' as ten (which is what they had decided with their teacher).

NEIL Ten. That's ten?
ROBERT I know it isn't really, but it's the equivalent because this number system's based on six and –
NEIL What do you mean? I suppose it's quite good but we can't get ... put it down on paper ... you know, man.

After about four minutes of meandering, the boys were losing concentration and appetite for the work, but the teacher came over.

ROBERT It's hard this, you know.
NEIL We can't put it on paper. We know what it is, but we can't put it on paper.
TEACHER Yes, that's what we are going to try to learn to do, to transfer thoughts from your head: communicate. One thing you could do is to make a list of your new words going down, and by the side make a list of the numbers as you would normally write them with the symbols.

ROBERT But you can't compare them because this is the number system up to six and our number system is based on ten. So you just can't compare it.

TEACHER Yes, but we've got words, haven't we? You're saying that your min is what?

ROBERT Well, it's equivalent to ten, or that's the last number before you go on.

NEIL It's not ten, though.

TEACHER If you go counting as you go, right, start counting in your system.

ROBERT In – that's nought – yin, sin, fin, pin, min.

TEACHER Min is which number?

ROBERT Five.

TEACHER What's the next number?

NEIL Ten.

TEACHER What's the next number in your system?

ROBERT The next number is yin-in.

TEACHER Is it?

ROBERT Yes.

TEACHER Yes, yin-in is six, but you're writing it down as a one and a nought.

NEIL Because in's a nought.

ROBERT Well, it's ten really.

TEACHER It's still the sixth number in your chart, isn't it, because you say it's like one-nought. So something must have happened to the column headings.

ROBERT They've changed round like an abacus.

TEACHER Yes, right.

ROBERT You get so far and you change round. It's like in an abacus.

NEIL Instead of going up to ten you only go up to five and then you change.

TEACHER Yes, fine. So make three columns: your counting system, the counting terms for what the number is in our ten system, and the symbols like your one and the nought.

The discursive, open-ended discussion, much of which had evolved out of the boys' own interests, led happily into writing, making a language for their mathematics so that they could communicate with an audience and remind themselves of what they had established.

Not all the mathematics in the school was like this work. The Head of Mathematics was aware of the constraints of working with experienced colleagues who thought and taught differently from himself, and with new teachers who had little experience of working in the ways I have described. One young teacher in the department was able to examine and change his practice as a result of being on the language and learning committee, as I mention later in reviewing the state of the language across the curriculum when I revisited the school in spring 1978.

Humanities

Humanities at School 1 concerns the first and second years and is an integrated course – in this case an integration of geography, history and social studies. It is taught in mixed-ability groups. The Head of History sees the *raison d'être* for an emphasis on integration as a shift of focus from subjects to be taught to skills and ideas to be acquired.

'Skills' was a term which I came across many times as the Language across the Curriculum Project rolled on, and it was a term about which I felt a lot of unease, largely because of its connotations of rote practising, which seems to have very little to do with understanding. However, I began to appreciate that it was a term which could re-direct one's focus away from, for example, history as a body of knowledge towards the children and the guidance one can offer to enable them to direct their own learning. For instance, at this school children were taught to use books as sources of information (which involved using an index and making notes); they were taught to find books in the library, to read maps, to look for and at primary evidence. Increasingly the Head of History had come to appreciate the course as an enterprise by which children could involve themselves with different life-styles and cultures and different ages. She was never satisfied with 'day in the life of' work, which is still the nearest many children get to entering imaginatively the history they are doing. She used Longmans' History Games very success-fully. First-years, after doing a study of their own village as it is today, went on to study a village in medieval England. One of their activities involved a meeting of townspeople to decide whether or not to have walls around their town. Each member of the class would take on a role (apprentice of the tanners' guild, runaway serf, etc.) and, in their role, would argue their case for or against building the wall. Later the department went on to devise their own games (see the 'Humanities revisited' section of this case study on p. 70), encouraging involvement yet always with an adequate basis of information to back up the enthusiasm and innovation of individual pupils.

The shape of the thinking behind the Humanities course had been influenced very much by the Head of History's involvement with the Schools Council History Project, which first led her to consider history as the collecting and interpreting of evidence and to an appreciation that history is what children do in lessons, not some separate corpus of knowledge which she must transmit, they receive. She and the participating departments came to re-write the Humanities course during the first phase of the school's concern with language issues, but without recognizing explicitly that they were re-shaping language activities in their lessons. At that time the Humanities team had felt that the language across the curriculum debate was not speaking to their interests and so they largely ignored it. But they were informally encouraged (by a particularly enthusiastic head) to appreciate the value of what they were doing in terms of language and learning and, in a later upsurge of activity at the school, they were to become more confident and articulate about their work.

Every department which sets about overhauling the ways it works seems inevitably to face a crisis of resources. History at this school was no exception. The department – and this statement could well be applied to many departments which I saw throughout the project – was making demands for new materials (and on materials already in existence) which could not adequately be met. Deciding to change your syllabus usually means involving yourself in a cottage industry of producing new material. It usually means, too, looking at the problem of children with reading difficulties. Lessons which offer more variety of activity inevitably offer more opportunities for getting lost. At the time of my first visit the department had enlisted some help from sixth-formers and from a remedial teacher who came into lessons and worked with children who also needed reading tuition.

In the Humanities lessons I saw, a first-year class was beginning a new topic. The children had covered their own village, then had gone on to study a medieval village, and were now going to look at a present-day Indian village. The teaching team had produced its own introductory booklet containing some general information (about contrasts of wealth and poverty, diversity of language and culture) and a number of jobs for everyone to do. These involved quite a bit of atlas work to re-establish the geography element in the Humanities course after the largely historical work on the medieval village. The first job was to find India on a world map in an atlas, and then colour it in a handout outline world map, then to label continents and oceans. The next job was to find in the atlas the countries surrounding India (a list was provided) and to mark these on the outline map. The work presented an interesting crop of difficulties:

SARAH That's the Arctic Ocean. We've done the Indian and the Pacific.

LOUISE Where's the Indian Ocean? I've not done it.

SARAH Yes, you have. Right now we've got to Atlantic Ocean ... Atlantic Ocean ... and that last one is the Pacific, the Pacific's round there.

LOUISE Round where? Round the corner bit?

SARAH 'Cos mind you I always forget that the world is round. Yes, because when you're looking at it on a map –

LOUISE Yes, and you know what that is? It's not part of America, it's the tail end of Asia. It's gone round the corner.

As I have said, this class had not done map work recently, and the girls needed to talk through what they were doing to remind themselves of what they knew of the conventions of maps. Having labelled the oceans and continents, they called over the teacher for a reminder about the next stage of the work.

TEACHER You haven't coloured in India.
SARAH Which is India? Oh yes, I see, that pointy bit.
TEACHER Look at your instructions.
SARAH Oh yes: 'Colour in India.'
TEACHER Well, you've got a title on your map so it's all right in fact.
SARAH There's India.
LOUISE Where's India? Where?
SARAH That pointy bit that we were worried about . . . that . . . look like that.
LOUISE Is that all India is? It's like a leaf.
SARAH But compared to England it's much bigger.
LOUISE What colour shall I do it?
SARAH It doesn't look much bigger than England, does it?

One of the illustrations in the booklet that everyone in the class had been given was a drawing of India with the British Isles drawn in black and placed inside India, so that with the two countries drawn on the same scale, the vast size of India could be suggested. The girls had not taken in that information or had forgotten it when they looked at their outline map, on which India was indeed very small and, on that very small-scale map, was not much bigger than England in absolute terms.

The problem of scale, or rather their failure to appreciate maps in terms of scale, stayed with them in their next job, which was to turn to a map of Asia in their atlas and to mark the countries surrounding India on a second outline map. The second map was of Asia rather than the world, and was on a different scale from the first outline.

SARAH [reading her instructions] 'Find the countries and mark them on the second outline map, China, Thailand, Tibet.' Right, we're going to find these.
LOUISE What's the first one? China first, which is where? Er-her, it's this part, look it's this part. I've got it, it's here.
SARAH What's that bit, then?
LOUISE Well, I've no idea really. All I know is that it's China there.
SARAH How do you know?
LOUISE Because look, there's the little bit, it's been marked off, and look, that's where it is on there.
SARAH There should be more. Well, if that's China there should be more there and there isn't . . . Miss P., where is China?
LOUISE I've marked it there.
SARAH Is that it there?

TEACHER Now what you've got to work out, you see, is that that map is on a much larger scale. Why don't you start off from what you've got in the middle, which is India, and work out from India.
SARAH Is that – oh I see, that bit's India.
LOUISE Where's India?
SARAH Oh, that whole bit's India.

In this intervention the teacher reintroduced the idea of scale without explaining it. The trouble for the girls was not in understanding what 'scale' literally means, but in using a sense of scale to find their way on their maps. One of them, Sarah, began to look at the map differently now that she realized there was a scale difference between the atlas map, her present outline map and her previous outline map. Louise took up the tip about 'working out from India'.

SARAH Where's China? We haven't put China on.
LOUISE No, and it's all up here because, look, there's no sea. This is China. I'm going to put it in.
SARAH If that scale's looking, it would be just Nepal and Tibet there. China wouldn't be on there.
LOUISE Let me just cross out the ones that aren't on here.

Later, after moving out and up from India and finding that several of the countries on their list were not indicated by boundary marks on the outline map, came:

SARAH What's that? That must be part of India.
LOUISE Wait a minute. Go up India a bit, go up India, that's part of West Pakistan.
SARAH Just put WP. I want to ask about that China thing, because if they're working from scale it wouldn't be on. What's all that down there?
LOUISE All that.
SARAH It's China. Is that China? Because if they haven't got those other countries on up here and if they're working to that scale of China, Tibet, China wouldn't be able to fit in, would it?

Although China did in fact figure on the outline map, there was much less of it than on the atlas map. Sarah did not get it right alone (and eventually asked), but she was beginning to make sense of the maps in front of her in terms of scale and to compare scales. Learning scale was not an immediate, unambiguous, once-and-for-all business. In the middle of her puzzled deliberations about China, Sarah could still say, 'I didn't expect India to be that big,' because now she was looking at a larger-scale map, just as before she had been surprised at how small India was (on the small-scale map).

Filling in an outline map of the countries surrounding India could have been a much speedier, tidier affair, possibly with the class copying the teacher's own map from the blackboard. Doing it in the way of this lesson, however, made possible a valuable exploration of uncertainty as well as eventual understanding. It also enabled the teacher to intervene in the girls' learning and offer them appropriate help. Working in groups of two or three, with jobs or materials in front of them, was a regular feature of the Humanities course, which helps to account for the readiness of these two girls to talk through their work together:

LOUISE We seem to enjoy it, though.

SARAH We find we get on.

LOUISE We feel more at home, though, working –

SARAH – together. It's much more fun and then you can both do it instead of working on your own. You can both share your news and see what the difference is.

LOUISE One person will know one thing and, you know, they won't understand something else and perhaps the other person will.

The course also included full-class discussion lessons. I observed one such lesson when the topic of India was being introduced. The teacher read to the entire class the first page of a booklet on India that all the pupils had been given. It was a brief account of the life of a village family. The overall question which the teacher asked at the end of her reading was: 'What are the main differences between your way of life and the way of life of the Indian family?' This stimulated a fairly straightforward activity, the collecting together by pupils of what they had heard and comparing it with what they knew from daily experience. The class pointed out differences in houses, food and schools, and seemed very interested in the status of women and girls in an Indian village community. A large part of the class contributed to a boisterous and good-natured discussion. This is an extract from it:

TEACHER Right, Richard.

RICHARD Nowadays people just go to work and then they'd have to grow their own crops and things and be self-sufficient, really.

TEACHER Right, that, and where did we come across that word before?

RICHARD The Good Life [naming a popular television comedy about getting 'back to nature' in Orpington].

VOICE Medieval times.

VOICE Motor mowers.

TEACHER [writing 'self-sufficient' on the board] What does it mean? It means The Good Life, it means the Middle Ages. What does it mean, David?

DAVID Provide for yourself.

TEACHER Yes, you've got to provide everything for yourself. So what does – self-depending upon yourself for providing everything – now what does Ran have to provide for her family?

It would be a mistake to think that a concern for pupils to formulate their own knowing leaves no place for whole-class get-togethers but only for small-group talk. There was a good energetic feeling to this occasion, lots of people chipping in, and it was skilfully conducted by the teacher, as the transcript shows. She took up those definitions of 'self-sufficient' – The Good Life and the Middle Ages – and she realized that the pupils who put them forward had the understanding but not quite the appropriate words to articulate that understanding. So she used what had been said to float her question again and get 'provide for yourself'. This does not necessarily mean that David, who said it, understood self-sufficiency better than Richard, who had said 'The Good Life', but it does mean that his understanding was in a more shareable form. The class went on to work in groups on the mapwork, some of which I have mentioned, and on a topic which they could choose from a list including: the role of women, home life, religion, the position of boys and girls, and marriage.

Finding resources was the team's chief bother at this time. Their thinking was ahead of most of the materials available, and at times they had to make do with second-hand matter – not always very well reproduced.

The writing which came out of the India topic was a disappointment to the teacher. It was very much the writing of second-hand experience, distanced and a little dull. In contrast was the writing which came out of a drama session organized for the entire first year, with the Drama and History Departments co-operating. 'Ug', stone-age man, and Leroy, space-age man, were placed in a circle representing the world. Aided by home-made props and loans from a local museum, a child representing Time moved round the circle showing when land, mammals, mountains and prehistoric animals appeared. At the appropriate time Ug arrived in a real bearskin, with a slide-show to illustrate his life. Time had to take just one pace, as opposed to walking round and round the circle, for Leroy to appear in 'space year', demonstrating what a short time humans had been on earth. Back in classrooms the children made a display about Ug's life and their own, consulting books and materials provided by the History Department. They did collages and wrote commentaries on them. Several wrote stories, one of which is reproduced below.

Ug meets Leroy

Ug had come forward in time, in fact into Leroy's world. He was standing in the middle of Trafalgar Square, just standing and looking amazed at the people. Somebody looked at him and went up to him, this somebody was a professor of early man and his name was Professor Stoneage. Ug held his spear tighter ready to attack this strange looking thing. Mr Stoneage thought is this fake or a real Stoneage man? He then said 'hello', but Ug just grunted then Mr Stoneage knew it wasn't a fake, he held his hands to show a peace sign and Ug understood because he smiled. Mr Stoneage said 'come on old chap better get you out of this place, come back to my house its just along the road. I think we'd better get a taxi otherwise we shall get some funny looks'. Mr Stoneage waved a taxi down and got in but Ug was scared of this hard object. Professor Stoneage understood and said 'Its all right it won't harm you' and he patted the seat. After a bit Ug understood and got in. The professor said to the taxi driver '23 Green Gate Road and go slow, please' the taxi driver said 'Right O'. Then they started to move. Ug grunted all the way home and he was glad to get out. Mr Stoneage fished out of his pocket the front door key and fitted in the lock, then the door opened he walked straight inside. A pale blue carpet and a open fire met Ug's eyes, Ug knew that a fire meant warmth and he was cold so he walked in, the warmth of the carpet was soft on his bare feet. Then the warmth of the fire met his face. He ran to the fire and warmed his hands, it was a lovely feeling. The professor then made signs to see if Ug was hungry, Ug nodded his head. Mr Stoneage went into the kitchen he did not know what to give Ug, but thought of the simple things like apples, bread, cheese, milk and meat but he cooked the meat so it was warm. The professor brought the food in on a tray. Ug leaped to him, and took some cheese but the professor shook his head and said 'Put that back old chap and sit down', and he pointed to a chair. Ug put the cheese back and sat on the soft springy thing. Mr Stoneage passed him some meat and bread. He did not give Ug any knives, forks or plates because he knew that Ug only wanted to eat, and would not understand knives, forks or plates. The food disappeared after 5 minutes but Ug was satisfied because he had a smile on his face. The next step was to have Ug to have a wash because he was very smelly so the Professor ran some water in the basin, Ug was willing to have a wash but he wasn't going to use this white slippery stuff, he looked much cleaner after this wash but the Professor thought that Ug couldn't wear his bearskins because they had fleas, and were very dirty. So Mr Stoneage found a clean old shirt and some striped trousers that he never did like. Ug smelt and touched these strange things, while Mr Stoneage put the trousers on. It was a funny feeling having something round your waist, then the shirt on one arm in two arms in button up the buttons and there you are a nice clean Ug. Ug thought the clothes were great but felt a bit funny. It was getting dark and the fire didn't give much light so the Professor turned on the lights, Ug wasnt scared because he was used to strange things happening. Mr Stoneage tried to teach Ug a few words he learnt fire, food and Professor. The progress that Ug made was very much improving and after a month Ug could talk like any modern man.

At the bottom of this piece the teacher added the comment: 'An excellent story, Louise. You have written it carefully and you have put in some thoughtful details.'

Occasions such as the drama morning and the writing which came from it have served to convince the departments of the need to involve children actively and inventively in their studies, and to give them room to follow up their own ideas.

Revisit

School 1 was the only school in the case studies for which there was time to make a return visit (in March 1978 after the earlier one in May 1977). Such a visit, I thought, could help to answer these questions: What did language across the curriculum look like in the school some eight months after my first visit? Had it been sustained or had it faded? Had it shifted in emphasis and, if so, in what ways?

THE LANGUAGE AND LEARNING COMMITTEE

The Language and Learning Committee, which it will be recalled had just formed in the summer of 1977, was composed so as to be representative of all the subject areas in the school. In all, the committee numbered about 10 per cent of the teaching staff. The deputy head was keen that the committee should develop as a body with the ability and credibility to make recommendations to the rest of the staff. After their first meeting, an encouraging but rather tense affair, the committee decided that their first priority was to find out more about what goes on in other's people's lessons, and to find out something of the children's views of their learning. The deputy then organized visits to lessons. Virtually everyone on the staff went to someone else's class for one lesson, with subsequent visits being arranged informally. For a number of staff the activity served to break down inhibitions in talking about teaching (especially teaching in other departments). It was something that the less relaxed and confident staff of two years before, at the beginning of the school's language across the curriculum work, would not have suggested. It was welcomed as a measure, however limited, that enabled teachers to talk from experience of other colleagues' lessons, rather than from speculative ignorance.

A second activity initiated by the very first meeting of the new Language and Learning Committee was the collecting of diaries by a number of the pupils. Pupils kept a diary of a week's lessons, some very fully and frankly, some very sketchily. Unfortunately, one member of the committee became particularly concerned about the status, validity and acceptability of such materials, on the grounds that they were 'subjective and impressionistic'. Remarks such as: 'This lesson is good because you have to work on your own and ask your own questions,' and 'I find it so frustrating when the teacher spends half the lesson explaining it to you and you still don't understand. But when I finally did understand it is so simple. Then when a girl has been away I explained it to her and it only took me about two minutes and she understood,' strike me as worthy of the most serious consideration, and it seems a pity that they should be discounted. Because these comments are personal (what else could they have been?) this does not make them invalid. In asking pupils to report on their own learning we must recognize that if we want to turn those reports into something other than personal statements then the onus is on us from the outset to provide the analytic framework into which they can be slotted – a step which mistakenly presupposes that we know what we want from pupils and have an already articulated theory of learning to help in obtaining it. If we ask for a diary or a set of impressions then it is our responsibility to treat these with the seriousness with which we would treat the comments of colleagues.

What proved to be a more profitable and far-reaching suggestion came later in the first term of the committee's life (summer 1977). It was proposed that the committee should look in detail at some area in the school where developments in teaching were taking place which deserved a wider audience, and about which the committee could make recommendations. One committee member suggested the Enquiry course, and as a result the leader of the Enquiry team prepared material and a talk about that work, looking at which took up two full sessions of the committee's time. The deputy head then made a suggestion to the committee in the following paper.

Language and Learning Committee

During the last two meetings the committee has looked at the kind of work that pupils have been doing in 'Enquiry' lessons this year and talking with staff who are teaching Enquiry about the aims, objectives and practice of the work. As with lots of other areas in the school, it has been felt that there is a considerable amount of common ground between faculties especially with regard to enquiry, or investigation, approaches towards learning in *the first year* and that it would be valuable for each faculty and/or department to discuss and, through its Language and Learning Committee member, to set out its approach in this field.

So, for the next committee meeting, faculty representatives have been asked to write an outline of the work in the faculty which falls under the umbrella of pupil investigative work and to duplicate copies of this outline for all committee members to be handed out and discussed at the meeting.

The outline should be set out under two headings:

1. *Teacher techniques and approaches* towards pupil investigative work (classroom methods, teaching strategies, use of small-group discussion, teacher direction, asking questions, etc.).

2. *The learning skills* we want pupils to acquire so that they are able to take increasing responsibility for their own, more independent learning (asking their own real questions, writing for audiences different from teacher organizing and sustaining work, examining evidence, etc.).

The potential values and dangers of such a proposal are perhaps obvious. A thoughtful department, guided by a thoughtful committee representative, could use the proposal to reflect on the teaching going on in their own area and to explore how this could be changed. But the way remains open for a less self-critical department to respond with the 'we do that already' rubric. By the time of my second visit to the school a number of departments had already produced their documents, and more were on their way. It looked like an impressive achievement for the new committee, which was still something less than two terms old. But I realized that neither the deputy head's optimism about the work of the committee nor all the paper that had been produced was adequate evidence that the language across the curriculum movement in the school had become a significant force.

Talking to the committee members gave me a fuller understanding of how they were seeing the Language and Learning Committee, whether they were able to take back to their departments what they learnt at committee meetings and whether they were able to modify their own work as a result of being on the committee. For the Boys' PE representative the talks about 'Enquiry' had helped him to become articulate about, and so clarify, his own teaching. He felt the importance, in his own teaching, of letting the child take over a problem, of encouraging him, say, to interpret the difficulty of balancing on his head as a problem of mechanics and geometry and to apply the principles grasped in this situation to a new one. He had come to appreciate, too, the importance of clarity in his own instructions. In teaching the breast stroke in swimming, for example, it is very important to ask: 'Is the water pressing against the inside of your leg or is it on top, against your thigh?' Without taking care to ask the swimmer to feel the water inside his leg the teacher may hinder the pupil's success. This kind of thing was what he took from the committee to his department, and in the regularly time-tabled department meetings he would report to his colleagues and open a discussion. This teacher valued the work of the committee highly. Listening to others had given him confidence in his own work, and he felt it was important that the committee had broken down barriers to communication between staff. 'There isn't integration in the staffroom,' he pointed out, explaining that members of most departments had their own corners in the staffroom. He found the meetings at which 'all the people you will talk to are from other departments' very worth while.

The language and learning representative from the Mathematics Department was also very positive about the achievements of the committee. For him the two concrete successes of the committee were (a) the statements from each department on investigative methods in their own subject areas, and (b) the suggestion (which had been taken up) for an in-service day conference of all staff. He was hopeful that out of the papers collected from the separate departments would come a school statement of guidelines for good investigative techniques and the reasons for teaching through developing the method of enquiry, with the committee serving as a clearing house for the operation. This teacher had consulted with his head of department about taking investigative methods into his own lessons and was learning about presenting pupils with problems (how to describe a point in a plane, say) and getting them to characterize it and formulate an answer for themselves rather than offering a recipe, and a language, for pupils simply to take over wholesale. He wasn't so sure, however, about how important the work of the committee had been to the rest of his department. He thought that his status as a very junior member of the department was a disadvantage. Certainly a department such as his, containing a number of strong and experienced teachers, could be a difficult one to shift to new ideas, whatever the seniority of the committee member involved.

A venture such as the Language and Learning Committee is particularly important to departments resistant to innovation, so long as it remains an active forum for alternative ideas. Not only had the Mathematics committee member been encouraged by his experience of the committee but several members of the Mathematics Department had also expressed an interest in joining subsequent Enquiry teams. From talking to those and other members of the Language and Learning Committee I got the impression that it had achieved considerable success. It had provided a platform for ideas that initially had been aired in the context of Enquiry work, which at that stage represented the most thoughtful and systematically scrutinized language and learning project in the school. At the same time it had given colleagues, particularly those in the committee, a sense of common purpose and of mutual respect.

'Enquiry' or 'investigative learning' had become the topic which enabled departments to talk across the curriculum. In the documents produced in response to the deputy head's discussion paper, 'Enquiry' principles were taken up through departmental interests (reading and interpreting large-scale maps from the geography element of Humanities; distinguishing between primary and secondary sources from the history element; skills and techniques appropriate to different materials in Creative Arts). When an in-service day conference for the entire staff of the school was suggested by the committee and subsequently held, it was organized through departments, with each department planning a day's activities (speakers, films, discussion sessions). Suggesting topics for general consideration, before giving them over to departments to be discussed and developed as appropriate, seemed a promising way forward for the committee.

The committee had taken its place at the centre of the school's work on the curriculum. It now had the confidence and respect not only of its members but of a large section of the staff. Behind its work was the determination of the head and deputy head to keep language and learning going.

HUMANITIES REVISITED

On my first visit to School 1 the main development on the Humanities course had been in encouraging pupils' own use of materials to investigate people of other times and cultures, as well as people of today. A continuing concern of the Humanities team had been to provide classes with more materials, particularly original sources, from which they could work. In their local village studies, first-year children had been able to work on census return sheets or village directories. The team were building up a bank of nineteenth-century census sheets from a particular year for all the villages in the school's catchment area. Children then could find a family – their names, ages, occupations (of the adults) and information about where the family had previously lived. Having chosen a family, the children then asked questions about the kind of life they had lived and could use other resources (still largely textbooks) to answer those questions. The participating departments had been helped in this work by a student teacher who had gone to the central Nottingham library and printed the census sheets out from microfilm. In preparation for their work on the census sheets pupils had done exercises drawn from the Schools Council Project on History, Geography and Social Science 8–13.[5] Using the census records one child had been able to trace a family through the village up to the present. Another, who had some old photographs of her village, used the directories to try to put a date to them. Working on 'My village today', one girl had read a local newspaper article about tradesmen and had used the census returns to find out who, if anyone, was doing current tradesmen's jobs 100 years ago. The emphasis in the year's village study had been on how much pupils could find out and what resources they themselves could bring in to school.

The more the departments had been able to provide resources the more they found they could get children to bring in relevant material – a particularly important activity which they had had no experience of in their primary schools.

For second-year children the History Department devised their own simulation game, based on Monopoly. The class, as medieval peasants, risked chance cards ('bad harvest', for example) and collected money if they passed 'harvest'. They had a map of their village and, as they gained land, they shaded in their maps. At a suitable stage the game was stopped and teacher (as enclosures commissioner) fed in information about enclosures and set up group discussions of villages to decide whether or not they wanted enclosures. Enclosures were made, the game started up again, and landless labourers emerged. They had to sell up and move to the towns. Members of the department generally felt that the game had brought children to understand the enclosure movement as a set of problems affecting many people's lives, rather than as a set of remote facts about events that happened long ago. Similarly the information provided by the 'improvement cards' in the game ('Jethro Tull's seeding machine', for example) had meaning in terms of the livelihood of a group of people, and didn't simply supply another name linked with another invention – which is, I suspect, how most of us remember the Agrarian Revolution.

Children in the third year studying the Home Front in the Second World War were, like the first-years in their village studies, encouraged to provide their own resources. And they did, bringing to school ration books, newspapers, gas masks and other memorabilia from the period. The Home Front work led to their producing a newspaper, with groups of children choosing and investigating a particular topic and being encouraged to do their own research. There was still pressure, though, for the History Department to find and provide resources, with no special resource-building or planning time allocated within the school day. An investigation of the way of life of people from other times or places cannot just conveniently happen out of nothing and will be dependent upon the quality of resources that can be made available. Recognition of this led the department to spend their time during the in-service day conference devising a simulation game on the opening up of Africa by explorers, a move supported by the Language and Learning Committee, who saw their concern with adequate resources for investigative learning as particularly apt at that stage.

ENQUIRY REVISITED

The other departmental development I followed up on my return visit to the school was Enquiry, because it had had such an influence on the Language and Learning Committee. When I talked to the teacher who was in overall charge of the Enquiry project he told me how the pilot work of the previous year had grown into the new year's course. His Enquiry pair (himself and a science teacher), and indeed most of the other pairs, has been able to take advantage of their freedom from usual syllabus constraints – not having to cover a chunk of 'content'. They had been able to let pupils decide on a topic for themselves and come up against the brick walls of inappropriateness, lack of resources and so on – to discover, for instance, that they could do little direct investigation in school into satellites or dolphins. The pairs met together regularly to share accounts of what their groups were doing. They found out that a number of children, particularly more able boys, asked questions which they could not answer through Enquiry techniques and so would have to turn to books and to reading and copying, a way of working that looked increasingly unexciting as other pupils' enquiries got underway. But the Enquiry leader felt confident enough to let a number of his pupils make false starts, realize that they had made inappropriate choices and start again. 'When should we intervene?' became the question that most concerned all the Enquiry teachers in their meetings.

The following (uncorrected) piece of self-contained, self-motivated work on worms was a good example to focus on. Mark's diary describes his first false start on a topic with 'postage', the way in which he moved from the library books he had found to suggest his own experiment and also displays the tenacity of his interest. The Enquiry teachers were able to take his work and use it as a model for other pupils to see what a successful Enquiry looked like. Mark's teacher for Enquiry was also his English teacher. He was particularly struck by the differences he observed in him in the two kinds of lesson. In English Mark had always written short pieces and, although alert in discussion lessons, had displayed no taste for the sustained organized work he had produced in Enquiry. It was a difference still puzzling his teacher.

Earth Worms

There are two sorts of earth worms common in England but all togeather there are 6 breeds.

How The Worm Burrows

An earth worm moves along by gripping with its rear and streaching foreward and then gripping with its frount and curling back. The worm gets extra grip by sticking out briscles on its under side. For each segment it has 4 briscles but there are non on the first and last segment. It moves the soil to the sides as well as eating some of it.

[Diagram: 'A Section of A Worm', showing 'Briscles', 'The Central Gut', 'Nerves']

Sencing fom moles
A worm can sence when a mole is near by the vibrations it gives off when digging. This makes the worms surface in the same way as it does when you stick a pole in the ground and twiddel it about.

My thirey of why worms surface when it rains
My thirey of why worms surface when it rains is to do with them being abel to detect when a mole is near. They detecth when a mole is near by vibrations it gives off and they surface to stop them from being eaten. My thirey is that the rain gives off the same vibration and the worms sence better on the under side so they would think its a mole under them and surface.

OR IS IT?
Because they sence it's wet and come up for a wash or a drink.

My Wormery
I made my wormery going. sand soil sand soil ect. The attual room the soil takes up is $1\frac{1}{2} \times 32 \times 24$ cm. On the front there is a see through Plastic screwed to a wooden frame with wooden legs.

[Diagram: 'MY WORMERY']

Exactly 1 hour later one of the worms got 13 cm deep. The other worms just beried them selfes in the first layer of soil

[Diagram: 'MY WORMERY ONE WEEK LATER (AFTER MADE) front and back']

Why My Worms Died
I accidently left my wormery for 4 days with out any warter. When I discovery this I took the side off to see if any were surviveing. I found 1 and that was dead. (It HAD 7 IN IT)
The other 6 must have died and decayed.

Earth Worms Names And Types
Earth worms are some times called natures plough men *WHY*
They are proberly called natures plough men because
They
PLOUGH MEN = Because they do a simular job to a plough man turning the soil and letting the air in to the ground.
NATURE'S = Because they are natural.

Why Earth Worms Like It Wet
Earth worms like it wet because if it's dry they srivel up and die and if they don't die it makes digging very hard.

[Diagrams: 'A PIECE OF NORMAL SOIL', 'A PIECE OF CAST SOIL']

After a piece of soil has past a worms digestive system and come up on to the surface it is called cast soil. (The cast soil has a lot less humus and other various things that form the normal soil.)

Dairy

Week 1
Discusion. What Enquiry realy means. (Assembly)

Week 2
Decide on postage get folders Ask Questions get started useing books.

Week 3
Decide postage wont work: to hard and to Big. Decide to do worms: out digging worms with neil had row split up start work useing books

Week 4
Use different books from libary keeping on worms

Week 5
Bring along worms make minuture wormery whacthing them (boring) get book again going on from how they move to them sencing from moles.

Week 6
Got a thirey about worms worte it up. Got to get a wormery made at home and allso a tin can sprinkler. To do experiment with it.

Week 7
Made wormery useing sand soil sand soil ect. Warterd it coverd it with paper makeing it dark going to start experiment with tin can and warter. No conclusion, tin can had to many holes in it, flooded the hole aera no good next week going to try again with less holes.

wormery
After worms had been in the wormery for about 1 hour one got 13 cm deep and the rest just beried them selves in the top layer of soil.
Next week copy up.
Warterd on thursday and friday and monday and thursday

Week 8
Rained can't do experiment on tin can and surfaceing. Soil in wormery gone down 3 cm top up with sand needed. Next week earths plough men and types, Why they like it wet. Wormery taken home more soil and sand to be added.

Week 9
For gotten wormery (alough they all died lack of warter) Got to bring next week to proberly refill (if not done about casts and natures plough men if it wet) Next week got to finish off Why My Worms Died.

Week 10

finished wormery (WORMS) TOPIC DONE ABOUT EVREY Think I
wanted/going to start new topic on some thing I can observe/CORN/How we
get differnt sorts How It harvested what it's made into and how it's differnt

GET WHEAT BARLEY AND OATS IF POSSIBLE
PICTURES OF A COMBINE

1. HOW WE GET DIFFERENT TYPES OF CORN.
2. WHATS THE DIFFERENCE
3. HOW ITS GROWN (And harvested)
4. HOW IT GETS TO THE FACTORY
5. HOW IT'S TURNED IN TO FLOUR (in the factory)
6. MADE IN TO BREAD

In setting up Enquiry as they had done, the team had arranged not
just to teach but to monitor their teaching as well. They were not at all
self-congratulatory about their work. The team leader was still concerned about the amount of time-wasting that was going on, an extra
risk when a teacher is not simply 'putting a class down to work'. He was
concerned, too, about the children who just wanted to copy from books.
But alongside these problems came an increasing number of competent
yet very individual enquiries into, for example, horses, pigs, mice and
roses. At the centre of team discussions still remained the problem of
when to intervene and of how to make that intervention an invitation to
the child to take his or her work further, rather than an instruction
about what to do next.

A criticism sometimes made of curriculum ventures such as Enquiry is
that, because their concern is with learning to learn and not with what is
being learned, they cannot be taken seriously as models for teaching
under normal conditions. It is argued that they really side-step the constraints of time and syllabus that circumscribe in their everyday work.
The positive value of Enquiry is clearly appreciated, though, by staff at
School 1 where the debate which sprang from the experiment provided
the Language and Learning Committee with its first major advance: a
discussion of the applicability of investigative learning principles across
the curriculum. As a result, a number of teachers from other departments asked to join the following year's Enquiry team. Providing a space
for experimental work such as this is a rare achievement. It enabled a
number of teachers with a common interest to make a commitment to
the new curriculum work and to monitor and document it. Starting off
by involving just two departments it eventually, by articulating with the
Language and Learning Committee, spread across the curriculum. A
school-based, teacher-organized activity such as this seems to be much

more than just second best to the kind of in-service course which LEAs might provide if they had the funds.

References

1. The materials for this project were published for the Schools Council by Holmes McDougall, Edinburgh, 1976.
2. Published by Macmillan Education, 1977.
3. See E. Lunzer and K. Gardner, *The Effective Use of Reading*, Heinemann Educational for the Schools Council, 1979.
4. *A Language for Life*, HMSO, 1975, p. 50.
5. *Place, Time and Society 8–13*, materials from the Schools Council Project on History, Geography and Social Science 8–13, published by Collins Education, Glasgow, and ESL Bristol, 1975.

III.   Case study 2

Of School 2 the headmaster writes: 'The school is situated eight miles from the centre of Sheffield. Its catchment area is mixed, ranging from mining villages and agricultural areas to a further development of Sheffield suburbia with substantial areas of council housing and increasing development of private housing. Our pupils are drawn from eight different junior schools ... We ask our junior schools to give us friendship groupings of two to three pupils so that every child entering the school will go into a group containing at least one friend. The junior schools are then asked to provide a subjective grade based not on objective tests, but on what the class teacher feels may be the pupil's ultimate potential on an A to E scale, where C is thought to be average. These grades are purely for the purposes of setting up truly mixed-ability groups and are never referred to again during the life of the child at this school.

'A liaison teacher is employed partially to aid the transition to secondary school of the pupil, but essentially to gain the maximum information possible on each individual child. He collects this information formally from junior school staff, and more informally by being present as an observer and assistant in lessons, or by interviewing and testing individual children who may have social or educational problems of which we should be aware and on which we can act.'

For the purposes of this report, the most important area of the liaison teacher's work is concerned with the diagnosis of reading and comprehension problems. In the final year at the junior school each child is tested in reading. School 2 runs an in-service course to improve standards of diagnosis and remedy for poor readers identified in this test. The school also has an Integrated Studies course in the first year, which displaces traditional English, History and Geography, where the child's use and experience of language is monitored by one teacher. Each of these teachers accepts the potential benefit implicit in integration through one teacher supervising a year group over an extended time and across several 'subjects', and has undertaken a separate in-service course on the diagnosis, recording and remedy of reading weaknesses. They feel

76

that their awareness of language usage is heightened by the experience, particularly when teaching subject areas outside their own professional training.

The Language Policy Working Party

At School 2, as at School 1, a deputy head was appointed, part of whose brief was to develop language and learning in the school. During my visit, the school was coming to the end of its first year of sustained work in this area. Almost from the start of that year the school had had a language policy working party, members being invited by the deputy head to ensure representation of a range of subjects and degrees of seniority. He reckoned that language across the curriculum often seemed to be a vague and ungraspable topic and therefore, very soon, uninteresting. With this anxiety in mind he set up the working party's first assignment. At the end of the school year the books of six first-year children were collected: two of top ability, two of middle, two of low. Members of the working party set about counting the numbers of words which those children had written during that first year of their secondary schooling. Generally, members worked in pairs and looked at subjects other than their own so that they could become aware of what happened elsewhere. The deputy head was making what he felt would be a critical first move: revealing that the school had a language and learning problem, and trying to put it in perspective by stimulating a general discussion of areas of responsibility.

After counting, the words were classified into three broad kinds: creative work; personal observation and interpretation of facts; and copying from blackboard or book, or dictation. The broadness of the categories caused some ambiguity and meetings were held to establish criteria for ascribing a piece of work to a particular category. Of the 203 275 words, which was the total for the six children's work, the exercise showed that a staggering 95 525 had been copied or dictated. It also showed, to the surprise of some members, that English did not involve children in the most writing. The results, when circulated by the working party, caused dismay and hostility amongst the staff – perhaps not unexpectedly. The evidence that a lot of copying or dictation was going on was taken to be an accusation of bad teaching and thus a threat rather than a suggestion that a balance between types of writing is everyone's concern. At this stage, however, language across the curriculum had come to seem a much less nebulous issue.

The hostility gradually abated as the working party went ahead with a year's meetings. The deputy head wanted teachers to feel that they were learning about language in these meetings and that they were being offered something that they could take to their own teaching. Cloze procedure (in which every sixth, eighth or twelfth word is deleted from a piece of text, and pupils, singly or in small groups, fill in the missing words to restore the sense of the passage), prediction and sequencing were discussed and used in practical sessions, with the teachers doing the exercises to be set to children. Sometimes similar sessions were then arranged for departments. For instance, the deputy head did cloze work with the Mathematics and Science Departments, using geography textbooks, so that the teachers did not have the advantage of their own expert knowledge, thus allowing them to experience the difficulties of using contextual clues and finding accurate and appropriate words. This kind of technique can sensitize teachers to what it is they are asking children to do when they ask them to read (and encourage them to face the embarrassing fact that we are not very sure what goes on when we say: 'Read this.'); and it can offer them a strategy to take into their classrooms. As a result a couple of members of the Science Department did introduce cloze procedure to their classes.

In further meetings the working party looked at pupil/teacher interaction by listening to an anonymous tape from a primary school, provided by the local adviser. After meetings of this kind members of the group became confident enough to experiment with their teaching and willing to share their experiences with colleagues. For example, a Humanities teacher decided to teach the 'same' topic – a Stone Age community – differently to two different groups, each a first-year mixed-ability group, to assess the relative effectiveness of two methods. The idea was to make the first approach very factual and formal, to treat the teaching of history as a matter of conveying information. For the second approach, history was regarded as an exercise in empathy and imagination, an idea often discussed by the department and one influenced by the Schools Council History 13–16 Project. In this view, the study of history is regarded as an imaginative reconstruction of the past, using evidence to begin and to shape the reconstruction.

Almost the first thing that the teacher working with the two groups realized was that his idea of a formal lesson was not necessarily that of the group he was teaching. Part of the formality of the approach was to use an overhead projector to display notes during a lecture lesson. This particular group had never seen an overhead projector before and the teacher sensed their excitement and their enthusiasm for the new equipment. I am not arguing that there is a necessary connection between formality and dullness, that because this lesson was lively it could not have been formal. Rather, part of what we mean by 'imaginative involvement' is the kind of enthusiasm for the use of resources and materials shown by a group who in this case were meant to be more distant from and objective towards their topic.

Written work from the two groups was collected and taken along to the working party. Here the discussion was inconclusive, although it produced the striking comment that the different arrangements for the two groups had not really produced significantly different results. The children who had been invited to write imaginatively seemed to be using their stories as a vehicle, sometimes an awkward one, to tell everything they knew about Stone Age people, rather than as an opportunity to transpose themselves imaginatively into an alien community. Here a number of questions suggest themselves. Were the materials available for the 'imaginative' approach particularly imaginatively produced? The 'dispassionate' group also had access to the same film strip, and in addition a Radio Sheffield tape of a journey into pre-history and two reference books, *From Early Man to Norman Times*[1] and *Men Become Civilized.*[2] Apart from the tape, the material had not been made to encourage a vivid sense of the past. But pedestrian material can be turned to imaginative use and even the comprehending of cold facts involves some exercise of the imagination.

The Humanitites teacher and his colleagues on the working party were familiar with the term 'expressive writing'.[3] For them it seemed to imply that one should let children write stories and poems as a natural and spontaneous expression of what they know, rather than making them write in more formal (and probably unfamiliar) language. The problem is that asking a child to transform experiences he or she has been told about or has read about into his or her own language is not an untutored activity easily stimulated by the invitation: 'Tell a story.'

TAPE-RECORDING AND LISTENING

At a further meeting of the working party which I was able to attend, the group discussed a tape transcript made by an education research student in a chemistry lesson. Briefly, the tape illustrated the struggle between teacher and taught when a teacher and a class see the same thing but have different explanations for it, and when the teacher wants to manoeuvre the group to see what he or she is seeing. This kind of session, a group of colleagues listening to a tape and scrutinizing a transcript of one of their number in class, can lead to some of the most productive and insightful work in language and learning. It is more difficult than collecting pieces of written work for discussion, yet most teachers would feel that the heart of their teaching lies in those numerous verbal exchanges, with large or small groups or with individuals, when they try to get things across, to find out where pupils are at and to see if they have understood. The collecting and monitoring of classroom talk is the essential work, and unfortunately the donkey work, of language across the curriculum, because it provides a direct opportunity for teachers to learn about 'the linguistic processes by which their pupils acquire information and understanding' and to appreciate 'the implications for the teacher's own use of language'[4] from the immediate example of one's own or a colleague's classroom. A sensible way to begin this work seems to be to collect information about what is already being done, and to try to account for apparent successes and failures in language terms. What a teacher brings to the analysis, the frame of reference imposed on the taped raw materials, will naturally vary with his or her differing interests and knowledge.

Outside agencies

In the summer of 1975 a group of HMIs had visited eight local schools which had already shown an interest in the Bullock Report. At this stage none of the schools had an appointee responsible for language policy work. The point of the visits was for the HMIs to form impressions of what was happening and report back to representatives from the schools – the heads and some of their senior members of staff. The minutes of the reporting-back sessions have a familiar sound to them: teachers did too much talking; written work was handed in to be proof-read by teachers and was generally not regarded as providing an opportunity for the teacher to monitor and foster the child's learning; little was being done successfully to encourage children to read widely. The newly appointed local adviser for English had recently made what he described as a 'whistle-stop tour' in the authority, giving talks to raise issues and set the scene for further language policy work.

I do not underestimate such work by HMIs or by local advisers. Meetings of groups of schools, or of single schools addressed by speakers with the qualities of compassion and clarity, can serve to arouse considerable concern and enthusiasm. Perhaps the disappointment from such meetings is that very rarely will there be continuing and sustained support. As the reader of this book may surmise, the number of schools going it alone with difficulty is far too high.

Integrated Studies

During my visit to School 2 in summer 1977 the first-years were being taught in mixed-ability groups on an integrated history/geography course. There are probably as many versions of integration as there are integrated courses. At this school the integrating is done via the teacher, i.e. one teacher is responsible for the history and geography work of one or two first-year groups. The first-years spend roughly two terms exploring historical and geographical aspects of 'Living Together' and a third term on 'Communicating Together'. The work in Integrated Studies that has been mentioned already (the two ways of studying Stone Age people) illustrates the thinking of, and the difficulties encountered by, the department at this stage. There was a commitment to an empathetic, adaptive approach to historical situations and an appreciation that the approach was going to require new ways of working with language; but at the time of my visit stereotyped worksheet handouts were a regular feature of lessons. The worksheet is a fairly recent and already somewhat suspect resource, but it has quite a persistent presence in many classrooms, nevertheless. Although there are many kinds of worksheets, one or two general warnings can be made about them. They will almost certainly have a set of points or questions which, by the way they are worded and sequenced, will represent a fairly tight structure for learning what somebody else has already learned. In the case of worksheets in this department there was usually a sequence of questions on a few pages from a textbook – a structured guide to a structured guide. As an effective way of enabling groups of children to move, through exploratory talk, from what they understand already into new understandings, such worksheets would seem inappropriate. This is not to make a naïve plea for children to be given no guidance or framework to bring to the materials with which they are to work, but to suggest that the guidance of most worksheets is too rigid, and assumes that learning is neatly linear and is the same for everybody. Consider, for example, the appeal to imaginative engagement with the history and geography of Lincoln made by the following worksheet.

Introduction to Lincoln

1. Draw a map showing the site of Lincoln. (p. 8)
2. Explain why the present-day street pattern is different from the Roman street pattern. (p. 11)

3. *The Market*

    (a) How far do farmers travel to the market? (p. 15)

    (b) How did they use to travel to market, and how do they travel today? (p. 15)

    (c) Describe the provisions market. (p. 18)

    (d) What is meant by a 'sphere of influence'? (p. 20)

    (e) Name some towns in Lincoln's sphere of influence. (p. 20)

4. *Work*

    (a) Draw a graph showing what people do in Lincoln. (p. 21)

    (b) What jobs are done by people working in the services? (p. 21)

    (c) Why did the engineering industry develop? (pp. 22–3)

    (d) Make a list of heavy industrial firms, and say what they make.

    (e) Give some examples of light industry in Lincoln. (p. 26)

    (f) Look at the plan on p. 21. Attempt to explain the location of the industries.

In a first-year lesson I tape-recorded two girls who were working on this worksheet.

PUPIL 1 What is meant by a sif, serfia of influence, sphere of influence? Page twenty, copy it off there.

PUPIL 2 Shurrup.

PUPIL 1 Twenty. [*Reading*] 'On the map on page fifteen dairy farm which cattle are sent be sold at the cattle market has been shaded in on this map you will see that the area . . . have called this a sphere of influence this map on page . . . shows.'

PUPIL 2 We don't –

PUPIL 1 I know but it doesn't tell you what it is. Mr F. has told us but I forget, that sphere's round or summat. It's got influence. Should I put my hand up?

PUPIL 2 [*reading*] 'If you joined all these places together . . .'

PUPIL 1 [*reading*] 'A sphere of influence is a shaded area,' because it says there, 'and shaded area this would have another sphere.'

PUPIL 1 'And shaded area . . .'

PUPIL 2 'Name some towns in Lincoln's sphere of influence, above, page twenty.'

PUPIL 1 What's it say?

PUPIL 2 'Name some towns . . .'

PUPIL 1 Cattle market.

PUPIL 2 Yes, farm.

PUPIL 1 Towns isn't a farm.

PUPIL 2 Stallholders. I don't get it. Provisions market.

PUPIL 1 It's got to be in here somewhere.

PUPIL 2 This is it, towns. These are all of them, aren't they?

PUPIL 1 Don't know.

PUPIL 2 I'm sure it's that Market Rasen.

The question which the girls are tackling here is probably the most difficult one on the sheet. Their difficulty largely arises because of the phrase 'sphere of influence', a very posh expression to describe a fairly straightforward idea – especially for children living in villages or small communities on the outskirts of a large town. But the girls are working conscientiously and not unintelligently in spite of their difficulties, using the textbook as a source of clues for their answers. It is the kind of exercise, I would argue, that we should want children to do occasionally as practice in using and reading textbooks. Clue-hunting is a useful strategy. As a staple in an educational diet it is inadequate.

The materials produced by the department show how difficult it was for these teachers to abandon the style and model of the textbook. The opening page of their course handbook, *Sheffield: The Growth of the City and its Steel Industries*, reads: 'Between 1400 and 1700 Sheffield developed cutlery trades based on local ironstone, charcoal and water power producing lines of settlements along the valleys of the Don, Sheaf, Porter and Rivelin. In the late eighteenth century the introduction of steam engines made industry (and housing) concentrate in the town centre, where coal was brought by canal.'

One's worries about this from a language point of view are those one would have about much textbook material (and if one came across this passage out of context one would probably assume that it came from a textbook). The language seems unnecessarily obtuse, 'developed cutlery trades' and 'introduction of steam engines' disguising really quite simple information. More importantly it represents a view of history which the department were trying to move away from: history as a specialist body of knowledge to be transmitted, in suitably specialist language. Reading the passage, it would be difficult to imagine that it was intended for children, many of whom know the Sheffield area and all of whom will have had experience of railways, canals, houses and factories and of change in their environment. All this knowledge and experience, some of it very direct and concrete, is the kind of resource from which the children might make their own imaginative reconstruction of this particular past, if given the right encouragement.

The teachers seemed not to be trusting their own declared commitment, remaining suspicious of activities that did not look like 'work': building models, making plays, etc. Instead of being recognized as central to the work of understanding, such projects were offered as treats at the end of topics. Below is a very brief extract from a drama session about machine-breakers. The boys were reading and re-making their play as they went along, working from a script, checking that names of characters were right and stopping occasionally to question the sense of the play. It is not possible for me to identify individuals – some of the group used more than one voice, to indicate different characters.

[*Reading the play – as a cue*] What's he want?
What's he want?
Come to join the gang.
I want to come and join the gang.
All right. Leave us.
What's thy name?
Somebody get the book out.
Wagger.
No, Ragg.
Thomas Wagger.
Ragg.
Ragg leaves.
Why does Ragg leave, anyway?
He's left the room to let them talk.
Oh, aye.
Ragg leaves the room.
And then Oliver says, I want to join or I'm oft to't government.
I want to . . . [*The scribe of the group writes this as a line for the play.*]
Nay, don't say go to government because then they'll know he's a government spy, won't they?
So I want to join your gang.
They'd kill him, wouldn't they?
I know what you're up to.

The boys slipped in and out of role with bewildering ease as they simultaneously made and criticized their play. The scribe conscientiously wrote and prompted. The group sustained this work for an hour with an impressive concern for historical accuracy and for plausibility in the way individuals behave. The textbook which provided the background for their work did not seem particularly engaging at first sight, but among the commentary were lots of extracts from diaries and contemporary accounts which these boys had selected and used resourcefully. Now I am not suggesting that history or integrated history/geography should consist of a series of scripted plays, but the extract does pose questions about which language activities may best enable children to realize an understanding of the topics they are studying.

On a first-year day visit to Lincoln the approach to take seemed less problematic. Each child had a sheaf of worksheets, but this time their use and layout were appropriate because they directed attention to details of townscape and architecture that could easily have been missed. There was time and the evidence for them to see how the city had grown and changed, and to sit locked in the cubicles of the castle chapel experiencing the discomfort and isolation inflicted on prisoners in the name of religion.

Maybe the (sometimes unperceived) tension between ambitions and practices in language work would ease in the following academic year, when the English Department planned to join teachers from History and Geography to offer an English/history/geography course integrated via the teacher. The history/geography teachers were hoping that pupils would then produce the kinds of imaginative writing more readily associated with English than with their own subjects and which might be fostered by the expertise of English teachers. Nevertheless, the stifling of English by the materials and ways of writing that were still most commonly used in Integrated Studies – a textbook passage plus comprehension worksheet – also remained a possible outcome.

Science

The science taught to the first two years (in mixed-ability groups) was an adaptation of the Nuffield Combined Science course. The two chemists who taught this course were also members of the Language Policy Working Party. As a result of this contact the head of department had reappraised the style and use of worksheets in chemistry, a subject which is often heavily dependent on them. Indeed when he first came to the school, in the middle of a year, he found that 'There was a third-year course running which was entirely worksheets and the kids could literally walk in, pick up a worksheet and never talk to me except for the purpose of finding a piece of apparatus . . . I was a child-minder.' Worksheets, he felt, were no substitute for teaching or for group discussion, and the Language Policy Working Party simply confirmed him in this view. The two staff teaching chemistry for Combined Science had become more specifically committed to enabling children to experience a variety of language uses in their science lessons, because they felt that the rigidity of worksheets, or of requiring written work to be presented in one formal way, might prevent a child from showing what he or she understands.

In the Report of the I L E A Oracy Project [5] I comment on the work of a child who wrote of magnesium: 'It conduct electricity very good because we put it by the electricity peg and then we put it by the wire and then it did light the bulb,' and who wrote of his salt and water solution experiment: 'When we put the salt and water mixed in to a little dish and we heat it up the water dried after about ten minutes we were heating it and the water dry out and the salt remain in the dish.' A group of teachers speculated about what would happen if we made up a sort of multiple-choice completion question for a child like that. He would not understand 'when a length of conductor is placed between two terminals' – because he talked about an electric peg. As one of the teachers said, imagining him confronted with 'When a salt solution is placed in an evaporating basin and heated, the salt is separated by evaporation – stroke – conduction – stroke – distillation': 'He wouldn't have a clue, and in fact he'd know the science.' This little example reminds us of one of the key principles behind an appeal to let a child use his or her own language. Quite simply it is the way that we most readily express our understanding: what we know *is* our language, and forcing an alien language on us may well make us appear ignorant when we are not. A scientific concept may be easily summarized or encapsulated by technical terminology, but often a preliminary grasp of the principles involved is available without the esoteric vocabulary.

The first science lesson I went into in School 2 (first year, mixed ability) came as an unusual experience. The room was darkened; children were gathered together watching a sequence of projected slides, views from a spaceship approaching a distant planet. Their teacher was re-minding them of the planet's crisis: insect life was dead, the human-like population was in danger of starvation unless new ways of pollination could be found. By the light from the projector the teacher then read three of the stories which were the previous week's science homework. This imaginative writing was more successful than the Stone Age man stories had been, and I think it is important to try to see why. First of all, the children were not simply being asked to reproduce what they knew in story form, they were being asked to imagine themselves as scientists faced with a real dilemma. On the day their homework was set they had seen the slides and been told about the grievous plight of the planet Zeta – a powerful stimulus to their creativity. The children also knew that some of their stories would be read out.

The opening to this lesson came towards the end of a sequence of work on plants. The children's books showed the range of activities which the work had involved. In some of these language was not appar-ently central (the class had taken apart flowers, identified their parts, looked at them through a magnifying glass and drawn what they had seen). Yet alongside Sharon's drawings were her carefully recorded obser-vations: 'Through the eyeglass the petal has got veins,' and 'This is not the actual size of the stamen it is three colours, yellow, brown and green.' In another piece of work the class had been invited to report on their seed-growing experiments. Sharon put in a lot of detail. Reading her account I was reminded of the great emphasis placed on careful and detailed observation in this first-year course. She also used diagram and words to complement each other – a fairly sophisticated device. 'We fixed our apparatus together like this,' she wrote, and had done a drawing of the glass-fronted seed sandwich she had made, saving 100 words. The writing was rather formal, with even the occasional passive. But her nice observations reinforced the point that her studied, impartial writing did not denote estrangement from the subject.

There was a cloze procedure exercise, too. In this case, from a short passage on 'How seeds are made' every eighth word was deleted. In groups the children had to work out an appropriate word for each space. At first glance this kind of thing may look no different from the old gap-filling exercise. The danger of gap-filling has always been that it leads to nothing more than a fairly mindless guessing game. Cloze can work differently from that, largely by being set up differently. Here children were asked to work in groups and encouraged to debate their decisions. Importantly, too, the passage came at the end of the children's investigations (dissections and discussions) of the parts of flowers and their functions in seed-making, so that it was a chance for them to revise and collect together what they had already learned.

Another activity involved the children, again in groups, in putting a set of words in order. These were the words: growing seed, fertilization, plant dies, pollination, mature plant, seed, plant withers, seed dispersal. It isn't easy to know where to begin in such an activity. There is no clear starting point in a cycle, as the initial doubts of one group I tape-recorded illustrate:

PUPIL I It's fertilation. It must be.
PUPIL 2 It must be mature plant. I mean, it's got to fertilize before you start.
PUPIL I Sir, is it seeds, young plants and fertilation?
TEACHER Right, well, put it down then, it's seeds.
PUPIL I Seeds.
PUPIL 2 Growing seeds.
PUPIL I I've put fertilation next.
TEACHER It's seeds, then what did we say?
PUPIL 2 Growing seeds.
TEACHER That makes sense, doesn't it? Seeds, then the seeds growing.
PUPIL 2 Then young flower.
TEACHER It's going to turn into a young plant and then a young plant is going to turn into a mature plant, and what did we say that meant?
VOICES When it's ready to die.
  No, when it's ready to breed.
  When it's fully grown.

TEACHER Yes, when it's fully grown, so are you on the right track now? Anyway, put it down, you can always put it right later.

I mentioned earlier the problem, in introducing children to scientific ideas, that technical terms may simply get in the way. This is not an argument for not introducing children to such language, but rather for an appreciation of how they can come to handle new concepts without the initial burden of the detailed explanation of terminology. Here, the children were not completely at ease with their understanding of the terms or of the processes to which the terms refer, but they had an overall sense of what their work was about (the teacher reassuring them rather than putting them right) and the job here gave them an opportunity to extend that understanding: working together, exchanging ideas, and not being tested. Whoever we are, learning something new and difficult does not happen instantly, and an exercise such as this recognizes that we may need to practice and consolidate learning.

After studying the life-cycle of plants and flowers, the group went on to study human reproduction. The idea may well bring a wry smile to the face of the reader, but from my observations it seemed a sensible sequencing of learning rather than a coy move from bees to people. The teacher was able to suggest analogies between the ovary, seeds and pollen of the flowers and the male and female reproductive organs. The children could bring to these lessons not just what they already knew or half knew from elsewhere but also their more recent scientific knowledge. In one lesson, after the class had seen a television programme on reproduction, the teacher gave each pupil a piece of paper soaked in a chemical which one either can or cannot taste according to one's genetic make-up. Earlier in the discussion about sperms and eggs one boy, David, had said, 'One half of the knowledge was male and one half was female,' picking up the one fairly brief reference to genes in the programme. The test with the paper revealed that some members of the class tasted nothing whereas others experienced a very strong bitter taste.

TEACHER The thing is, some people can taste the chemical there and some can't. How do you explain that some people can?
PUPIL 1 Some people are more sensitive than others.
TEACHER Possibly.
PUPIL 2 Since people have got bigger taste buds, it just –
PUPIL 3 – depends where you put it on your tongue.
TEACHER No, it doesn't. On these people who haven't tasted the paper I could put it anywhere on their tongue and they wouldn't taste it. No, I think Kevin was on the right track. Why is it that some people can taste and some can't?
PUPIL 4 'Cos everybody's different.

TEACHER Everybody is different, yes, good, but that doesn't really answer the question.
PUPIL 5 Summat to do with your parents.
TEACHER Yes.
PUPIL 5 Between your mum and dad you've got two different taste buds. Your dad could have one ... and your mother could have summat that couldn't taste it.

Even the most sensitive teachers can end up making the children play 'guess what is in my head'. The link between the reference to genes in the TV programme and the tasting experiment was more obvious to the teacher than to the class, who could not handle the fairly open 'How do you explain ...?' The transcript highlights the problem of wanting a class to talk speculatively but along one line. Interestingly, however, a number of the children's speculations were biological in *intent*, showing that the children had a shrewd notion of what counts as an answer in a science lesson. The teacher at this stage was relying simply on their memory of one detail in a film, and on their seeing the relevance of that detail to his question. When it was established that the class should look at differences passed on by parents, they talked about some of those differences (the ability to curl one's tongue in a certain way, for example). The discussion then continued:

TEACHER You see Sara – picking on poor old Sara! – you see her hair is curly, isn't it, whereas David's is straight. Why do you think her hair is curly?
PUPIL You don't take after your mum and dad.
SARA I don't take after my mum and dad.
TEACHER You don't.
SARA No.
TEACHER That's interesting, isn't it, because you must have got your curly hair from them, though.
SARA My mum and dad's hair don't – my mum's hair won't curl even if you put rollers in it.
PUPIL No, it's dead straight.
TEACHER That's interesting, isn't it, but they must have passed that information on to you.
PUPIL How do you know it's not her father.
TEACHER He hasn't got curly hair.
PUPIL It might be her grandad.
TEACHER Hang on just a minute, look, now there's Sara whose got curly hair. Right, now: her parents haven't got curly hair ... but she's got the information from them and that just goes to show that we don't look identical to our parents, otherwise we'd all look the same, wouldn't we? They pass on information to us that affects the way we look, but it probably makes us look different to what they are.

PUPIL We'd still be looking like Adam and Eve.
PUPIL How come I've got blonde hair and neither my mum or dad have?
PUPIL You've took after yourself. I'm fat like my dad.
TEACHER Because they've passed on this information in the sperm and the egg and that's made you and in that sperm and in that egg was something that said blonde hair.
PUPIL A list with blonde hair.
TEACHER Yes, that's right, a list of things in the sperm, and list of things in the egg that sort of made you and said what you look like.

At this stage of the lesson the children were generating ideas at a number of different levels and pushing them out into the general discussion. Some were realizing that there is something in family resemblances but that it may not be straightforward: 'It might be her grandad'; 'You've took after yourself. I'm fat like my dad.' One child realized that we can't just end up looking like our parents: 'We'd still be looking like Adam and Eve'; and the child who remarked: 'A list with blonde hair,' was beginning to make sense of the process of genetic transmission. It says a great deal for the teacher that such easy thinking aloud went on.

It had something to do with his personal qualities, but not everything. He had very skilfully called upon a common experience of family likeness and let the pupils explore a difficult idea from the basis of that experience. 'Genes' and 'heredity' had not been mentioned, yet this is what the conversation was about. Towards the end of the lesson the teacher turned to a pot of seedlings. The class quickly moved into revising the work on vegetative reproduction and its human analogue.

TEACHER Did you notice this, by the way? We just left that in that experiment.
PUPIL Whose is it?
TEACHER We've just left it and they've all sort of come up one by one. Should we leave them and see how they grow?
PUPIL I They'll grow big.
PUPIL What are they?
PUPIL I They'll grow that big.
TEACHER They'll grow big and then make more of their own kind.
PUPIL What are they?
VOICES They'll grow big, seeds fall off and make some more.
GIRL [her voice comes through other voices] Our Billy's growing cabbages and it rained the other day and it squashed all his babbies ... he went ... it squashed all his babbies into t'soil ... he went mad ... he calls his plants his babbies ... he always has to see his babbies before he goes to bed ... squashed his babbies, his little plants ... that's what my brother calls his plants, you know, his babbies.

What I have tried to illustrate in this account of Combined Science at

School 2 were some of the things that happened when a teacher decided that he wanted to break away from a pattern of worksheet and experiment, and (through the Language Policy Working Party) found the interest and gained the confidence to introduce a range of activities. He was particularly interested in encouraging the children to write stories, but this was something he did fairly infrequently and with a level of preparation of which 'Planet Zeta' is typical. He introduced cloze, a group reading activity, as a way for children to cope with the difficulties of textbooks. He allowed the children to organize their own write-ups of experiments. But perhaps most important of all, he had made the lab a place in which children readily worked together, talking through their work as a class. These children seemed to understand that the teacher's invitation to them to express their science openly, speculatively and imaginatively was a genuine one.

Problems and prospects

What had impressed me about the year's work at School 2, much of which became known to me through reports and accounts from the deputy head or members of the working party, was the range and variety of topics considered and a realistic concern to keep the topics practically relevant. At best, this had provided teachers with new understandings and gave them something to take into class and do. Yet, in spite of this, I felt that the working party had little sense of direction. Possibly the variety which at first seemed so stimulating was at fault here. No one topic had, at that stage, suggested itself as the one which needed deeper and further consideration.

At an informal meeting of the working party the head, a regular attender, talked about his aspirations for the first year of language across the curriculum. He had inaugurated the work feeling that a school policy initiated by himself and demanded of his staff would be counter-productive. 'People should see the need for it themselves,' he said. He summed up what he had wanted to achieve at the end of the first year of consistent work: a viable working party which

i could see the point of having a language policy,
ii had achieved some self-education, and
iii had broken the ice as far as listening to teachers teaching was concerned.

He went on to say that there was no clear direction forward. He felt that perhaps the working party had become too comfortable, and had achieved its measure of ease and confidence because it had worked largely on self-education rather than on influencing the staff at large.

We came here to a dilemma that was experienced by working parties in all the schools I visited. Reports from colleagues in other schools suggest that it is a common dilemma. However a working party has been set up, either by invitation from the head or deputy, by election or by asking for volunteers, most of its members would probably admit to more enthusiasm than expertise, and would want the working party, in its initial stages at least, to be essentially a self-educating body. What most people seem to underestimate is how long they are going to go on feeling uncertain about the character and value of 'Bullock work', still not able to give very much guidance to other colleagues, let alone make curriculum recommendations. Another set of problems often presented to school language policy committees, caught between a desire to find out and a desire to disseminate their findings or just unsure of the way forward, is the articulation of their work with school and local authority power structures and with the national examination system.

Language policy work demands more time of already hard-pressed teachers, and generally LEAs, though not this one in particular, go on refusing to take the recommendation for a language across the curriculum policy with anything like the seriousness that they have taken up, say, assessment. The idea that you can only do language policy work yourself, that it involves a personal transformation of awareness, can here be used as a mean excuse for not giving the kind of help and money which can provide the opportunities for teachers to learn from each other. Maybe the key issue is 'consciousness-raising', but there are easier and more difficult ways of doing it.

Most members of School 2's Language Policy Working Party now felt that they were inviting a wider range of talking and writing from the children, and a number of them worried that perhaps the relative openness of work in the first two years was inappropriate for the later years. The head, in a school heavily committed to CSE, was aware of the irony of offering an examination which, although it could be made to invite a more enquiring, less fact-grabbing approach to learning, was nationally undervalued. The worry about external examinations remains a very real and general one and is probably one of the main reasons why most experimental curriculum work, including the kind of reflection and revision advocated in the Bullock Report, takes place in the first two years of secondary school. As a worry expressed by teachers committed to looking at language and learning it is one that should be taken seriously and not dismissed as an excuse in bad faith for carrying on burrowing through a textbook and dictating notes.

One of the things which such a language working party could still do is to look at the often excessive examination load placed on pupils, bearing in mind the experience of teachers who have found that working thoughtfully with language takes longer than copying notes. To the group at School 2 the deputy head gave a salutary reminder that perhaps they need not be too concerned that the staff were setting overmuch imaginative, enjoyable work which aroused enthusiasm but which was a poor preparation for the scholastic grindery to come. He recalled their survey of the previous year, which had shown nearly half of the writing done by the first-year children sampled to be copying or dictation.

The working party, although it had been at work for a year and had made progress in terms of the head's three criteria, did not seem to be influencing many other teachers. It was interesting to note that the two departments which claimed to have been most influenced by the working party each had two members on it who could take what they had learned in the working party and could then work together on the needs of their own subjects. Amongst the staff generally one did not sense much concern or interest in the Bullock work, or anything of the threat that the writing report from a year ago had generated. The deputy head with effective responsibility for the curriculum seemed particularly concerned that moves in a language policy should come up from the departments rather than be imposed by him as the head's representative in this work. Both he and the head were concerned about the work of a number of departments which showed little concern for the needs of the mixed-ability groups being taught and little or no interest in language and learning. The head was sending two deputies into the problem departments to discuss mixed ability, teaching materials and methods. His deputy in charge of curriculum and language across the curriculum seemed to feel some reluctance to do this and some uncertainty about his role.

The situation brings into focus a problem not just specific to this school, nor to language policies, but embedded in wider questions of authority and responsibility in schools. Any head is seen to be responsible for 'the school', and heads of departments are seen as responsible to the head for the teaching in their departments; but there seems to be little clarity about the responsibilities of the deputy head and where he or she fits into the 'chain of command'. The deputy head in charge of curriculum in School 1 had pointed out to me that, ideally, someone in his post should *not* think of himself just as expert in a particular subject area. But almost inevitably his preparation for the responsibilities of deputy headship will have been as a subject expert, a department head. He will have to learn to see the school as a whole and to appreciate differences in the needs of different departments. Initially he has no right to expect allegiance from anyone and will have to earn the commitment of colleagues to the work he initiates. Recalling this talk suggested a number of explanations for the success and the problems of the language work at School 2. It seemed to me that the volunteer nature of the school's language policy, whilst having been good for the working party's confidence, was preventing it from becoming an influence in the school. The deputy head, I felt, needed now to ask for a more formal acknowledgement of the working party's responsibility to and need for contact with departments, and for a commitment from heads of department to concern themselves with the language work. He needed to make clear this mutual dependence (possibly in the way in which the deputy at School 1 had done in the later stages of his school's language work – see p. 65) and to emphasize his and the head's desire for language across the curriculum work to continue and to become more influential. Already the head had seen some of the implications of Bullock for relationships and discipline in the school: for example, an assembly could well be a take-a-part story with everyone joining in with words and actions rather than a homily from a dais. He had decided also to restructure the timetable to make fewer, longer teaching periods which would provide more suitable stretches of time for effective language work. Such moves suggested to me that language across the curriculum as an optional, voluntary activity was coming to an end and that its importance as the school's central curriculum issue would be reflected in a new role for its working party – perhaps with a chance of becoming a forum for curriculum development in the school. If that might sound too ambitious, then the group could well continue devoting sessions to listening to tapes of themselves at work, or looking at the writing they were asking of children, implementing what they had learned and shared together over the previous year by bringing it to bear critically on their everyday practices. I can appreciate that this may sound too legislative to those who believe that language across the curriculum must not be imposed by a head or his deputies, but must rather come from a staff who see a need for language policy; but, as both School 2 and School 1 came to realize, it is important to find a way of organizing a language policy that is not dependent on either a voluntary committee without clear articulations with the rest of the school at one extreme, or, on the other hand, on a series of edicts from the head.

References

1. J. Salt and F. Purnell, *From Early Man to Norman Times*, Oliver & Boyd, Edinburgh, 1970.
2. Trevor Cairns, *Men Become Civilized*, Cambridge University Press, 1969.
3. For the use of this term, see for example J. Britton *et al.*, *The Development of Writing Abilities (11–18)* (Schools Council Research Studies), Macmillan Education, 1975.
4. *A Language for Life* [The Bullock Report], HMSO, 1975, p. 529.
5. Irene Robertson in Rachael Farrar and John Richmond (eds.), *How Talking is Learning*, ILEA, 1980.

IV. Case study 3

School 3 is an all-girls school of 1630 pupils. In years one to three mixed-ability teaching is the norm. Options, taken up in year four, are limited because each girl does English, mathematics, a science, a language study, a craft, P E, careers and a personal development course. The school's catchment area, on the edge of an industrial city, is divided about equally between owner-occupied and council housing, the owner-occupying families being described by the head as 'first-generation middle class'. There lingers a not unfamiliar idea that education for girls is not of paramount importance, and although parents will be concerned with their daughters' education their main interest will be in seeing them equipped for a good job by the age of 16. The school buildings themselves are examples of undistinguished modern school architecture, but one scarcely notices because they are set in very lovely grounds.

An extract from the school's handbook giving information about the organization of the school includes descriptions of the following staff meetings, advisory committees and working parties:

Consultative Committee
This consists of Head, Deputies, Heads of School and Year, Heads of Department and anyone else who is interested. It should be scheduled at least monthly on Monday at 4 p.m. and should finish at 6 p.m. at the latest.

Function. This is the policy-making body of the school. No new principle should be put into action that has not been fully discussed in Consultative. A brief summary of discussion and notice of decisions should go into the Bulletin.

Curriculum Working Party
Membership is open to all interested and it meets fortnightly on Wednesday for two terms of the year to work out curriculum development. The agenda is published at the beginning of the year and recommendations are presented to the Consultative Committee.

Language Policy Committee
This consists of cross-disciplinary groups who are examining areas of language use in order to help staff to a language policy.

A finance committee and other bodies are also described in detail.

The Language Policy Committee

The working of the school's Language Policy Committee (often referred to within the school as the 'Bullock Committee') and that committee's connections with the Curriculum Working Party are important elements in the school's language policy work.

The formation of the committee owed a lot to the school's co-operation with the curriculum development project of the local authority's teachers' centre. Shortly after the Bullock Report was published the headmistress consulted her head of English and decided to contact the curriculum development project director for his advice and support. Subsequently at the school's Consultative Committee it was decided that the head should choose three members of staff to be the school's first Bullock working committee and that in their initial work they should have the assistance of six girls. The Language Policy Committee in fact came to consist of three members of staff: a craft teacher, a sociologist and a mathematics teacher, chosen by the head to represent a range of seniority; and eight girls, two from each of the years one to four. They met the curriculum development director and talked about different kinds of teaching and learning. The idea of the committee at this stage was to find out about current practice in the school and the curriculum development director suggested that a questionnaire would be a good way of finding out. The committee teachers and the girls agreed to work on one.

The Language Policy Committee reported back its proposals to the Consultative Committee and experienced strong opposition from a small number of staff who felt concerned about the use of girls in the work. The proposal, however, was backed by the head. Bearing in mind staff concern, it was decided that staff as well as girls should be invited to fill in the questionnaire. The questionnaire was piloted in July 1976 and used in the following autumn term. The teachers and pupils involved were invited to note the amount of time in each lesson devoted to: listening to the teacher, dictation, copying from the board, listening to other girls, listening to films or tapes, writing notes in rough books, writing notes or essays in books, working on projects, discussion in groups with teacher, discussion in groups without teacher, discussion in whole class with teacher, writing stories, solving problems, reading, tests, revision, experiments, practical work, visits, individual tuition. By this time one member of the Language Policy Committee had left the school and was replaced by a new member. Later in the year two more members were to join the committee because existing members felt that their group was too small. The ones who joined the committee did so because they were interested in its work but also because their free periods coincided with the committee's meetings. The original members had been given two extra free periods for their committee work. In September there were adjustments, too, in the pupil membership.

THE SCHOOL LANGUAGE POLICY SURVEY

Analysing the results of the questionnaire proved rather more difficult than devising it. The analysis displayed:

i percentage of time spent on a variety of activities by pupils;
ii a comparison of pupil replies with staff replies for the same activities;
iii a breakdown of staff replies by year.

Especially interesting were the findings that:

a both teachers and pupils reported large sections of time with 'teacher talking to whole class' and noted relatively little 'discussion'.
b 'The way in which pupils defined the various categories differed greatly from teachers' definitions.' There was an 'overall difference between what teachers and pupils think is happening'.

The survey had an open rather than specific aim: to make as many people as possible aware of 'Bullock work' and its field of interest, as well as offering an impressionistic view of patterns of learning and teaching in the school. It was, however, a piece of work which could have resulted in considerable hostility. Probably because in the stages of devising the work the Language Policy Committee had sought staff opinion (through the Consultative Committee) and taken heed of it, hostility was averted.

An almost immediate outcome of the survey was a request from the Curriculum Working Party (membership open to all) for the Language Policy Committee to look at the question of homework. Concern had been expressed about the third year and the adequacy of teachers' preparation of girls who would be moving into examination courses in their fourth year. In response to this concern a group of girls from the third year, whose tutor was a member of the Language Policy Committee, wrote full details of homework set and done over a three-week period. A number of fourth-year girls supplied evidence of fourth-year homework. This homework report, which is reproduced in full in Appendix A, was delivered to the head, who passed it to the Consultative Committee and thence to heads of department for discussion in departments. The head made a summary of comments she had collected from departments and published them in the school bulletin. The head also rewrote the section on homework for the staff handbook (her policy and practice guide for the entire school) as a result of the survey. An extract from the section appears in Appendix B.

Less officially, the Language Policy Committee was concerned to involve parents in the question of homework. They took the idea to the Consultative Committee, who agreed that tutors should use their time with tutor groups to find out what girls and parents thought of homework. It was felt that having a parents' meeting would get the opinions of relatively few parents. This way, although informal, could quite possibly put staff in touch with much more parental opinion. The Consultative Committee agreed, too, that a handbook on homework should be prepared and given to parents of each new first-year intake.

FIRST LANGUAGE POLICY MOVES

It seems worth while to sum up the work of the Language Policy Committee so far. The teaching and homework surveys represent one kind of 'Bullock work' not since repeated at the school. At this stage in the committee's life, according to the evidence of their informal minutes of meetings, the members were beginning to ask questions considered by many language policy committees: 'Where do we go from here?' and 'How do we involve more staff?'

A survey of language practices in schools is often one of the first jobs a language policy committee does. One cannot legislate for what such a survey should include because this will depend upon what a particular committee feels is feasible in its school, which in turn will be determined by the committee's own interests (a sociologist member may well enable a committee to be fairly ambitious in its survey) and by what the committee feels to be the general level of awareness and interest already in the school.

A number of questions can usefully be asked of a survey:

i Does it investigate the points you wish it to focus on as briefly as possible? (E.g., you can probably learn as much by following round one pupil for a week as you can by following round four; you can probably learn as much in three days as in a week.)

ii Is the survey simply going to raise anxieties or also rally interest?

iii Is it going to be something from which teachers and pupils can learn (see School 4's survey and its place in language across the curriculum)?

iv Will it give heads of department something to take up with their departments?

The constant two-way traffic between the Language Policy Committee and the Consultative Committee and the latter and the head may appear as cumbersome bureaucracy. In fact it served to articulate the work of the Language Policy Committee with the established policy-making procedures in the school and to give 'Bullock work' a central place in curriculum development. The Language Policy Committee, it should be remembered, was made up of three classroom teachers, yet it was consulted by the Curriculum Working Party (chaired by the deputy head in charge of timetable and curriculum). The surveys were typed up and published within the school, another indication that language policy work was being taken seriously.

When the homework survey was completed the Language Policy Committee wanted to give some feedback to the girls who had taken part. When the girls and the committee met the discussion shifted from the homework questionnaire and became a wider talk about the girls' experiences of being learners. Points from the discussion were again published within the school. This Language Policy Committee had been able to consider controversial issues and use these potentially controversial ways of working partly because it had been given prominence and status in the school.

FURTHER DEVELOPMENTS

When the original Language Policy Committee had been in existence for almost a year, it held an open staff meeting to discuss its work. The outcome of that meeting was that a second Bullock group was formed. At the time of my visit a third group, too, was getting under way. This happened because there was by now widespread interest in the school in the work of the original Language Policy Committee. The new groups formed as a result of this interest and because they had managed to find a time in the week when all of their members could meet. The deputy head agreed to keep this time free of other duties.

Meanwhile the original committee's work was changing in character. The topic they now decided to consider was classroom discussion and pupil talk. For the first time language itself was the central topic of their work, and for the first time, too, they had to look at the minutiae of teaching/learning. Members of the committee supplied tapes of their classes: a group discussion in Home Economics, and one-to-one tutoring in Craft. They were now beginning the slow business of self-criticism which all such groups seem to go through.

One trouble with classroom language work is that teachers can feel exposed in front of colleagues, who learn, probably for the first time, what their teaching is like. The classroom is very often a fine and private place, and it is easy to feel nervous when it is opened up. This committee had been working together long enough, and I would say productively enough, not to feel that way. But the group did not have such confidence in sharing their work with other colleagues. The sessions, they felt, were exploratory. The group worked from their own experiences and insights to make sense of and analyse the tapes.

Often the curriculum development project director was at the meetings. His role in language policy work had changed. Initially he had been instrumental in setting up the committee, suggesting that girls should feature in its work and suggesting the survey work. Now he would simply come along to meetings and join in discussion, but would never dominate, nor would he suggest a programme of work. It is true to say, however, that the original language policy group and the new one found his support invaluable.

The second Bullock group began to look at writing and its possible effectiveness in learning. They collected in books from a small number of fifth-year girls and looked at their writing in a range of subjects. They decided, too, to find out the girls' views on writing and its purposes (an indication that getting co-operation and opinions from pupils had become an integral part of their language policy work). This group, too, was keeping its work close to its chest.

At the time of my visit to the school the business of communication between the language policy groups and the rest of the staff had become contentious. In an open staff meeting it became a key topic. It emerged that if the purpose of dissemination to other staff was to form a general school language policy then none of the groups felt confident enough to do it. They were too uncertain about the direction of their work and particularly about the effectiveness of their ways of working. Certainly they were not in a position to provide certainties or answers to colleagues. At that stage they felt that perhaps the most they could do would be to circulate very brief statements of the questions being investigated by the various committees or by departments. By now the Home Economics Department was developing ideas under the influence of the head of department, who had joined the first language policy committee. The Physical Education Department, too, was carrying out a survey of its language practices. In spite of this activity, it was agreed that there was still considerable interest in language policy work which the committees were not tapping. Members of the committees in turn felt that their communicating with heads of departments and asking for feedback, which should have guaranteed keeping in touch with the entire staff, often did not work. It was suggested that use should be made of personal links between staff to bring more people into language policy work. One of the deputy heads was particularly concerned that the committees should regard themselves as having a duty to report regularly to the staff.

The problem had arisen because of a conflict in the demands made of the committees. The original committee, selected by the head, and implicitly the other committees, had been set up to work for and report back to the school as a whole. Indeed, the first year's work of the original committee was far-reaching in this respect. Yet its members felt that its most valuable outcome lay in the considerable amount they had learnt from each other, and it was their enthusiasm for this aspect that had led to the setting up of further language policy committees to act as seminar groups. They felt they needed the time and freedom to work out their own agendas and educate themselves, without demands for reports back to the staff.

My feeling is that there should be opportunity for both kinds of work. Even given the helpful support of the curriculum development project director and the head, there was still a great deal that staff concerned with language policy had to learn which could not yet readily or profitably be communicated to others. Perhaps the accusation that the language policy committees were ignoring the public aspects of their work were rather unfair at this time. After all, some staff on the language policy committees were also part of a sub-committee of the Curriculum Development Committee set up to consider assessment. Its brief included providing staff with information about various kinds of assessment with a view to helping the History Department measure the effectiveness of their new second-year syllabus. More directly concerned with language and learning, the original committee, some months after my visit, produced a booklet, *Making Choices: Selecting Appropriate Ways of Working*, in collaboration with the local teachers' centre. Four members of the committee had offered a range of ways of writing to their pupils, and in this pamphlet considered what resulted from that. It seems an important step to have taken and hopefully it will be the first of a number of publications which reflect upon and analyse actual practices of teachers in the school to offer them as models or illustrations to colleagues.

While the three language policy committees were meeting and considering their role, work on language in the classroom was already in progress in several departments including Physical Education, Science, Home Economics and History.

Physical Education

'How is it that some teachers do get involved with language policy and some do not?' is a question that regularly crops up. I cannot supply a general answer but can point out how the teachers I encountered became interested. The Head of P E at School 3, for example, became interested because she shared a lift to school with a member of the Language Policy Committee and became interested in hearing about language and the committee's work. It was my experience at this school that although there was a great deal of agonizing over dissemination of work and co-operation with more staff, there was such enthusiasm for language work that, informally, much was being shared.

Having become enthusiastic, what are the first moves to take? Many teachers feel particularly daunted by the prospect of developing this work in the classroom, and particularly uncertain of their own knowledge about language. The Head of P E started, sanely enough, from her own teaching. She made a framework for looking at language in her lessons, based not on language theory she had read but on her own practices. The framework she made is reproduced here:

Language in Physical Education

Teaching in a school which has recognized the importance of setting up active 'Language across the Curriculum' working groups, I found myself closely considering the forms of language used in teaching my own subject. Educational dance and gymnastics were those aspects of Physical Education on which I initially focused since they provided situations most conducive to study and observation in my school. (Most of my comments therefore relate to dance and gymnastics.)

What I have written is based on my own teaching experiences as well as more specifically on a series of dance lessons with a number of second-year classes (all girls). Although, ideally, a videotape recording of these lessons would have proved of great value, I was able to use a tape-recorder only, and therefore whilst teaching was very aware that non-verbal aspects could not be recorded, but only recalled by me afterwards. After each lesson I studied the recording, and at first attempted to analyse what I heard under the following points:

1. Overall spread of language used:

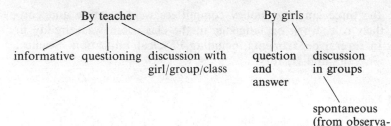

By teacher

informative   questioning   discussion with
girl/group/class

By girls

question
and
answer

discussion
in groups

spontaneous
(from observa-
tion, perhaps)

Is there a stress on any particular type?
Was the intention that there should be such a stress?
Were there the opportunities for the various types?

2. How is questioning made use of, and why?

e.g. for recall
development of ideas
reasoning
finding out background knowledge?

3. How is *observation* used, and follow-up comments, to reinforce learning?
Consider the type of verbal reaction gained after observation: do the girls
find it fairly easy, or do they need help in what to look for? How do the
comments from observers equate with what the 'movers' say they feel, want
to show, or are thinking about?

4. How is the class/individual informed of success, so that there is further
motivation?

5. Teacher terminology: How appropriate is it? Does it relate to everyday life?
Are explanations given or needed?

In using the framework to listen to tape-recordings of her lessons she
found that it was in some ways inadequate and added the following: 'As
I listened to the tapes, further questions arose.'

6. What *types* of talk are used?

e.g. to explain meaning, feeling or action.

Is one type used more than another in general, or is the type specific to the
lesson?

7. What is the effect of such talk? How well is teacher-talk alone found to be
effective?

8. Do misinterpretations occur? How are they recognized – through observation or talk perhaps?

9. Are certain terms/words used which, out of a PE context, mean something different to the class/individuals? If they are, is an association made so that there may be a fuller understanding?

10. How are problems in communication tackled by the teacher, e.g. in communicating ideas; developing a group idea which is lacking in creativity rather than group skill?

11. Are there similarities or differences between the language used in gym and that used in dance?

Point 6, for example, refines point 1. Generally the categories and questions in this second section are the more evaluative. The first section, though, enabled the teacher to collect and review language in her lesson and so to develop a more critical framework. She discussed the framework with her department and planned that, over a three-week period, three teachers would each tape two gym and two dance lessons with first- and second-year groups. These tape-recordings, with the framework, would then form the basis for more discussions.

Her main concern at this stage was the balance between talking (of whatever kind) in PE lessons, and practical activity. Was it possible to spend too much time talking in PE so that the girls performed badly, or less well than they could have done? A related set of concerns was the spacing and pacing of keynotes in a lesson. The keynote of a particular lesson could be an action, a movement flow, its direction, the heavy or light quality of the movement. Inevitably these became my concerns too, because I had to spend considerable time talking to the teacher about gymnastics and dance in order not to feel at a loss as I observed PE lessons. In other words, I needed my own framework for making sense of what I saw. In these discussions I learnt that 'gym is more purposeful, less self-expressive' than dance. In gym 'you relate to objects – in dance to your own body, to others, to the space around you.' What the two, gym and dance, share are movement principles which have to be understood intellectually and physically. In our discussions we pondered over the girl who could 'do' PE but might have no words for what she could do, or the girl who could explain movements but could not accomplish them.

Certainly, success in PE lessons is measured by bodily performance, which was why the Head of PE was particularly anxious not to spend too much time talking. It explains, too, why the other members of the

department were not over-enthusiastic to launch into language work in
PE. They were frank in saying that they could not appreciate the relevance of language policy to PE but nevertheless agreed to do the tape-
recording. They found, however, that they had been over-ambitious
about the number of tape-recordings they could make. PE lessons –
dance or gym – are difficult to record, and certainly it is very difficult to
get a recording of reasonable quality. It is also very easy to overestimate
how much tape one can cope with, particularly in the exploratory stages
of listening to teacher and pupils at work.

What follows is an account of one PE lesson – educational dance with
a second-year group. I found that from among the numerous recordings
I made in the department, just this one PE lesson provided me with
more than enough to say. At the time of my visit to the school, the plan
to tape lessons was just getting under way, so that I was in the position
of picking up one department's concerns with language and learning at
its very beginning. In this account I try to highlight and comment on
what, for me, were the salient language features in that particular lesson,
doing very much the same job as the PE Department were themselves
doing at that time. Like them I found myself leaving my initial framework when it would not cater for what I was interested in.

This particular lesson started familiarly enough with a warming-up
session. This involved the girls running and then leaping into the air.
After three leaps and with much clatter they rested.

The teacher, in the middle of the group, asked how the girls could
avoid overbalancing as they moved forward.

VOICES Go slower.
TEACHER Go a little more slowly, yes, so that will give you some time to control the jump up ... Will you think a little more now girls about lightness.
Even though you're going towards the floor you have to control and carry
your body weight. Think of all that weight coming close to the floor and then
you having to lift it all away from the floor. Therefore, am I going to get close
to the floor or not? Is it more important for me to get close to the floor or just
bend my knees a little bit?
    [*Inaudible answers.*]
TEACHER A little bit. [*Her voice is disbelieving.*]
VOICES Close to the floor.

Here we see another familiar situation: the teacher has cued the class to
give the right answer. Making a tape-recording is an excellent method of
becoming familiar with one's own ways of doing this kind of prompting.

    [*At the next brief pause.*]
TEACHER Stand where you are ... relax ... and just spring up and down on

your toes. Up down up down up down one two one two no heels and now begin to shoot the arms up and down [*demonstrates*] to shoot the arms up and down to shoot the arms up and down and really show that you're getting this lovely feeling of lightness. What part of your body does that really work very much?

VOICES Arms, arms and legs.

TEACHER Oh, I don't feel that I've got tired arms.

VOICES Legs.

TEACHER What part of your legs?

VOICES Ankles and calves.

TEACHER Ankles and calves, yes.

I was now asking what was the function of the question, 'What part of your body does that work very much?' Was it just an example of teacher playing at 'guess what's in my head', a game which we all play at times (and sometimes we even experience the embarrassment of realizing that we are doing it). Or did the question mean something like this: 'Get in touch with the part of your body that has worked and is paining you.' Was it, in other words, using language to increase an awareness and understanding of movement? I do not think this can be answered simply by an observer at a lesson, or by a reader reading what an observer has said about a lesson. It is something that could be asked and answered most fruitfully by the teacher concerned and by her colleagues. It seems an important consideration in PE, where a lot of teacher talk directs attention and awareness to parts of the body.

Having concentrated on lightness of movement, the teacher moved on to another keynote – the flow of movement through the body. All the time she demonstrated as she talked.

TEACHER Let's go back to a feeling of coming away from the floor. A movement that comes away from the floor. What I want you to start with, girls, is feeling, that is feeling that someone is pulling you gently at the knees then pulling you at the hips then at the chest and then at the head which is making you feel a movement that is passing through the body and you'll overbalance. I overbalance. I let the movement carry on – it wants to so I let it. So it's knees hips waist chest, have a go a few times. Just on your own.

[*They do.*]

TEACHER It's coming but you've got to slow it down.

This kind of talk and demonstration of movement by the teacher played a significant part in this and all the other gym and dance lessons I saw. On one level, judging the effectiveness of it seemed remarkably easy. One could watch the girls and see immediately how many of them had understood and had been able to put into practice the advice that the talk was offering. However, we were still left with our original questions: Do the girls feel that such talk is helpful? Could they do without it? Was the balance of talk and demonstration right?

After the girls had worked at movement flow there was another, longer pause in activity, this time with the girls sitting down in a fairly compact group. The talk changed, too, as the teacher deliberately began establishing connections between dance and things outside it.

TEACHER Can you tell me anything? You might be at home or you might be outside shopping. Something that you might see and you see the movement travelling through the body or through it in a similar way to the way you have just been moving.

The girls suggested: an action replay of a horse jumping, water through a hose-pipe, a cat arching its back, a horse's tail swishing, wrestlers falling. The connections were certainly there, and it now became the teacher's job to ask: 'What is the value in dance terms of making these connections?' Realizing these connections could encourage young dancers to appreciate a movement idea and so extend their own repertoire of movement. This is what the teacher was hoping for. On the other hand, the examples could simply provide the girls with particular actions to imitate, which in dance terms is not good.

At this stage of the lesson the teacher introduced a further keynote – body action, the actual movement in which the flow that the girls had been working on was being realized.

TEACHER Now thinking of these things will you go back and think of body actions. What the body does, like turning, rising, falling, opening, closing, and I want you to try and if you can concentrate on getting the movement starting in one part and travelling through to other parts.

Here the teacher did a turning, opening movement and asked the girls to call out which part was moving first.

There followed another movement session for the girls with the teacher talking as they moved, bringing their attention to flow and to body action.

TEACHER Where is it starting and where is it going through? Feel clearly where the movement starts and where it travels to – is there a winding up or an unwinding?

In our discussions together the Head of PE and I came to regard such talk as crucial. Its purpose, as I have mentioned earlier, is to put performers in touch with their own body movements and the expressive quality of those movements in order for them to develop and refine them.

[*At another break in activity, this time in front of a blackboard.*]
TEACHER Does anyone know, girls, what name we give to a movement which flows through the body like the one you have just been doing?
VOICES Flexible ... body wave.
TEACHER You often do a body move when the movement flows through in this particular way. I don't think you know the word – it's 'successive'. The movement flows through the whole body or part of the body successively. Successively. [*'Successive' and 'successively' were written on the board.*] For instance, if I lined you up and said I want you to ring, and you'd all got bells in your hands and I said I wanted you to ring the bells successively, what would I expect to hear?
VOICES One then the next.
TEACHER Yes – ding, ding, ding, ding, one after the other. Now what you've been doing is moving with successive flow. The flow through your body has been moving from one part to another, to another, to another. So you've been moving with successive flow. You've been moving successively. And what were the things you could tell me also move with successive flow? What can you see in normal everyday life?
VOICES A whip, sheets on a line.

The flow was the new keynote of the lesson, lightness or heaviness of movement, and body actions were keynotes that had been re-introduced, having been given separate attention in previous weeks. The girls had been encouraged to be light and to remember body action because these elements were being neglected in those early attempts to achieve flow. The way in which the teacher had introduced the new keynote struck me as exemplary and worth discussing with her. The girls, in this lesson, had spent considerable time practising making movement start in one part of the body and move through to other parts – at that stage without being told a name for what they were doing. During the lesson they had been encouraged to see how that movement happened elsewhere in things quite unconnected with their dance: horses, cats, washing on a line and so on. Later they were asked for their own words to describe that movement and gave 'flexible' and 'body wave'. At this point the teacher, realizing that the girls did not know the correct name in dance terms, but seeing that they understood the idea, offered 'successive' and 'successively' and supported this with the example of the bells.

The problem of specialist and technical language is often brought up in debates about language and learning. The answer to the problem does not, to my way of thinking, lie in simply providing children with lists of specialist keywords, but rather in collecting examples such as this, showing how and when such words might be introduced into the children's learning. This way puts the right emphasis on our teaching strategies. It now occurred to me to ask, 'Given that the girls understood successive flow, did they need the term?' I think that the answer was provided in the lesson. Previously they had been introduced to 'body action' and 'weight', both specialist dance terms, to which they were able to respond effectively. Teacher and class were building up together a dance language that enabled them to work together productively. But the terms had been introduced to the girls gradually and carefully after they had experiences and understandings into which to place the words.

During my visit the Head of PE and I decided to ask the girls themselves what they thought of the talk and demonstrations that go on in PE lessons. The Head of Department had a general talk with a class at the end of a lesson; I talked to two of the girls whom I had watched in the dance lesson. We both found that the girls seemed a little surprised at our question: of course – they declared – talking helped them, particularly if it was accompanied by a demonstration. Later, after the taping had been done and the Head of PE had listened to her tapes, she had further discussions with classes and produced an eight-page report on their views of physical education. I reproduce here part of that report.

'If you come across a problem in a PE lesson, something that you find difficult to do or to understand, how do you cope with it?'

Transcript from tape:

(1) GIRL 1 Keep on trying or ask a friend.
    GIRL 2 Ask the teacher to show you again and copy it.
    TEACHER But do you think the teacher always wants you to copy it?
    GIRL 3 No – take it in.
    TEACHER What do you do if you watch her, but still can't take it in – can't do it?
    GIRL 2 Have to keep really trying.
    GIRL 4 See what somebody else is doing.
    GIRL 5 That's not always good – she might be going wrong.
    GIRL 6 Stand and think for a minute and do it again.

(2) TEACHER Do you need to repeat something if you've done it well once?
    GIRL If you've got to be taught something it's not just to go out of your head when you've learned it – you've got to be able to grasp it. You've got to repeat it quite a few times.

None of the girls admitted to simply accepting the problem or to making no effort to solve it. They did, however, recognize that the learning process involves:

(a) practice and/or repetition	(practical)
(b) observation of demonstration, be it specific or random	(practical)
(c) thinking	(mental)
(d) questioning and talking	(mental)

The spontaneous answer to the question, from most classes, was as Girl 1 answered. Friends seem to be turned to initially, and then the teacher. When asked why, a number of girls said that often the teacher 'would tell us off for not listening'. Methods used by the majority of girls included:

(a) asking friend/teacher
(b) watching teacher/friend
(c) perseverance and practice through repetition.

The order of priority varied depending on the nature of what was being taught.

Relatively rarely do we ask pupils to give us their views on the education we offer them or their assessments of curriculum innovation. Yet, whenever the co-operation of pupils was sought (here and in the survey work at this school, when pupils were asked to write diaries at School 1) the pupils' responses were enlightening. It seems an aspect of language policy work which could well be pursued.

The PE work I have described here is a nice example of a homespun approach to language and learning. The teacher had no formal acquaintance with arguments about the role oof language in learning, yet she was perfectly well able to shape an initial framework with which to focus on the language in her lessons. She also appreciated that focusing is just the preliminary step. She and I spent a lot of time interpreting what had come into view. The tapes she made and worked on and the document on 'Pupils' views of PE' were the materials around which she and her department could begin to talk.

Science

The Head of Science at School 3 had, for a time, been a member of the school's original Language Policy Committee and had become a member of one of the new language groups set up later. Her involvement with language policy had meshed with several concerns about the teaching of science. Coming into the school as Head of Science, three years before my visit, her main interest had been to get rid of the over-neat and orderly (because untouched) prep rooms and laboratories, and to concentrate on practical work. A disappointing outcome of this move was that there seemed to be a gap between what the girls had done in lessons and their understanding of it. This was most clearly illustrated, for her, by remarks made by her sixth-form students, some of whom revised only their theory work for a written examination and had ignored their experiments on the grounds that such practical work could have no connection with a written examination. A further concern with learning, teaching and language centred on first- and second-year combined science. Mixed-ability grouping was introduced for lower-school science in order to break the pattern of expectations of performance which, the teacher felt, was imposed by streaming. To support herself and her department, which was not used to working with mixed-ability groups, she called on the curriculum development project director from the local teachers' centre, asking him to advise on teaching science to such groups. She felt that 'the department would be anti-Bullock because they didn't see it in their own framework', and so the request to the director was not that he should help with language but that he should help set up work in small groups. The Head of Science felt that 'in solving Bullock I would be solving mixed ability'. I mention this work to indicate the range of help available from the teachers' centre, and to show the range of concerns taken up in the department.

I was able to visit some third-year chemistry lessons where the teacher was involved with the first of the problems I have mentioned, the balance between experimental and non-experimental work (normally writing), and in thinking about the kinds of writing she was expecting girls to do. In order to help the girls understand their work more fully, the teacher was spending considerable time at the beginning of lessons on what could appear to be very traditional work. It matters, I feel, not to make an assumption that language policy work must involve 'progressive methods' (small groups, individual assignments or self-selected work with open everything from questions to windows). Anyone who has, for example, seen what fourth- and fifth-years will do with self-selected CSE project work will appreciate that the worst of practices (endless copying from ill-understood books) can result from unintelligent notions of pupil choice.

The beginning of a particular lesson, with a third-year top-ability group, made me appreciate the value of a getting-everyone-together session, with teacher very much in charge of proceedings. On this occasion the teacher handed back written work, which had been a set of questions on an experiment, and read out a piece that had been particularly successful. She then went over the questions. Her first question established that if an oxide turns litmus blue it is a basic oxide, if it turns litmus red it is an acidic oxide. One of the jobs in the previous week's homework was to compile a table of the oxides that had been used in class experiments. The table looked like this:

sodium	basic
carbon	acidic
magnesium	basic
sulphur	acidic

The teacher asked the girls to turn to their tables.

TEACHER The very last question was asking you to look at those results and try and discover whether or not there are different kinds of elements that form different kinds of oxides, and remember we mentioned if they end in 'ium' they were likely to be – what kind of element?
VOICE Basic. [*She mutters.*]
TEACHER What?
VOICE Basic.
TEACHER No, not basic.
ANOTHER VOICE A metal.
TEACHER Yes, a metal. Remember we had that list: calcium, barium, strontium. If it ends in 'ium' it's probably a metal. Can you notice now that sodium and magnesium are both metals and they both give basic oxides, carbon and sulphur are both non-metals and they both give acidic oxides. Right, let's have a little practice at that, then, to see if you've got the idea. What kind of oxide do you think potassium would form?
VOICE Basic.
TEACHER Basic. Julie, what type of oxide do you think nitrogen might form?
VOICE [*after a pause*] Acid.
TEACHER Audrey, what type of oxide do you think barium might form?
AUDREY Acid.
TEACHER Is she right, Pauline? Barium. Would barium form an acidic oxide?
AUDREY Basic.
TEACHER Do you think you're wrong, then? Why?
AUDREY The 'ium'.
TEACHER That's right, barium's a metal and therefore it's probably going to be a basic oxide.

The going was not easy. The girls had to appreciate that there are metal and non-metal elements (and they could not do this by observation – there is nothing in the appearance of those elements to relate to one's common-sense notions of what a metal looks like). Nor do the names give an immediate clue. The girls had to be told that 'ium' usually denotes a metal. They had to appreciate, too, that the elements produce oxides which are either basic or acidic, and that the metals (ending in 'ium') produce basic oxides and non-metals acidic oxides. Probably a reader unfamiliar with chemistry will have to read the preceding sentences particularly carefully, possibly more than once, that is, will have to do the kind of practising that the girls were doing in that lesson. Their experimental work alone could not have provided the information and categorization of results which such practising allowed.

Having appreciated the practice as a bit of necessary map-making, I should like to turn to the detail of some of the exchanges in the transcript. For instance, should that first response, 'basic', given as a reply to a question about an *element* (and wrong because it applies to an *oxide*) have been taken up and its wrongness explained, or ignored as it was, and the flow of the dialogue kept? Is the exchange after 'Is she right, Pauline?' an example of the teacher cueing pupils to give right answers rather than to air difficulties? I raise these questions because they pay the kinds of attention to the detail of exchanges that teachers working on language and learning often find most valuable. The teacher did, in fact, attend a fortnightly meeting of a small group of science teachers interested in language in science connected with Manchester Polytechnic. A detailed analysis of tapes was a key feature of those sessions. Working with tape-recordings can be invaluable, alerting one to one's practices, making one see what is going on in front of one's nose.

During my three weeks' visit to the school, the teacher and I, for different purposes, were collecting tape-recordings of small groups at work on their experiments. The clearest impression that the two of us formed, listening to those tapes, was how much effort and talk in lessons was devoted to the details and logistics of experimental work: chemicals and equipment being fetched and set up, test-tubes being washed between stages in an experiment, times being checked and recorded. The experiment *became* this kind of detail. This helped to explain, we felt, the state of sixth-formers who did not feel that experimental work had very much to do with their understanding of chemistry. Yet, obviously, it was not the teacher's intention that this should be so. Invariably, at the end of an experiment there were a number of written questions which called for an understanding of what the experiments had been about. These were written up for homework. Usually there was not time at the end of a lesson for the girls to talk in groups to work out answers to those questions and, as the tape-recordings showed, there was no opportunity in the middle of an experiment to consolidate understanding as well as doing the experiment.

One strategy to consolidate work, which I have mentioned, was to collect the class together at the beginning of a lesson, read out someone's work, and possibly have a question-and-answer session about the most difficult part of that work. Another strategy was to place greater emphasis on written work. In my second week at the school half the class, in groups, was working on thermal stability experiments, the other half on the reaction of carbonates with acids. The groups in each half were asked to write detailed descriptions of their methods so that in the following week, when the groups changed over, the thermal stability groups would be working from the instructions of the girls who had done those experiments in the previous week. The carbonate groups would similarly write up methods which the other half could follow.

In much of the discussion about language and learning the question of audience is recognized as important. Briefly, the argument is that very little of what children write in schools is read other than by a teacher proof-reading for accuracy and checking for adequacy. Providing different kinds of audiences might give children a sense of purpose in their work, a sense of responsibility for it. Reading work out to a class probably provides the easiest way of creating a new audience. The teacher was doing this regularly. Writing instructions for others to follow was another way. This first time it was not entirely successful because some girls did not provide sufficient detail for their readers. But it was an idea that could be developed.

Another central issue in the language across the curriculum debate has been that of 'specialist language' and the difficulties it may present to many children. At its crudest, the concern has been that big words are (inherently) difficult and so pupils should be introduced to them methodically, and the words should then be used consistently by a teacher and where possible by groups of teachers. The words are reckoned to matter because they encapsulate a specialism's key concepts. The temptation is to think that word equals concept, that in some way concepts exist separately from the conceptualizing that teachers or pupils do. The following may illustrate the problem. It is the beginning of an experiment on thermal stability done by one half of the third-year group already mentioned. The group had been given copies of a method sheet, the opening of which went like this:

Thermal Stability of Carbonates

When some metal carbonates are heated they break down (decompose). This is known as *thermal decomposition.*

You will be investigating a variety of carbonates and obtaining an order of stability. Those which decompose most quickly are the least thermally stable.

The teacher called together the groups (half the class) who were going to work on the experiment. The first job was to unravel the term 'thermal stability'. The girls were asked what 'thermal' meant; what did it suggest? Someone said 'thermos flask'; someone else said 'to do with heat'. They were asked next about 'stability'. Someone said 'strong'.

TEACHER Strong, no, I can be stable not strong. What happens if I stand up and I'm unstable?
VOICE You wobble.
TEACHER Not quite what we want here.

The expression 'thermal stability' is critical for understanding this passage and it seemed right that the teacher should spend time with the group establishing its meaning. It also seemed an excellent strategy to invite the girls to recall other contexts for 'thermal' and 'stability' which could provide a clue to its meaning in chemistry. In the case of 'thermal' they did this very successfully, but 'stability' became a problem, ironically enough, because the girls had a variety of very plausible meanings for the word.

The following week I taped a repeat of this session on the introduction to thermal stability, this time with the second group of girls. One girl took up the entire phrase and suggested 'how much heat it can stand up to', which the teacher acknowledged as a perfect definition. What interested me, in discussion with the teacher afterwards, was the wording of the method sheet. It seemed to be a kind of semantic hurdle, not necessary to the understanding of the science, and indeed getting in the way of understanding. The real value of the work on thermal stability was to do with establishing a valid experimental method or, in the very accurate terms of one of the girls, 'making the experiments fair', by keeping a constant flame, by timing accurately, by using the same amount of all the various carbonates. Yet in the introductory session far less time was spent on these details than on the word-chasing.

What the tape enabled us to do was to ask if the worksheet could have been written in more familiar language. Could the scientific term have been provided at the end when its meaning had already been established? Wasn't the girls' understanding of thermal stability dependent on careful experimental work and compiling and interpreting tables, not on being given a scientific term? The Head of Science was going on with tape-recording herself and her classes at work because it was providing a lot of information about how pupils were dealing with their work which needed this kind of puzzling over.

Interest among the rest of her department in such work was uneven. All of those teaching first- and second-years were working on group activities in Combined Science. At a couple of lunchtime working sessions, which I joined, the Head of Science and chemistry teachers went through a set of questions on an examination sheet to see if they had indeed asked the pupils to take up problems rather than give back information. Another scientist, a physicist, was taking up the idea of pupils writing for specific audiences. He was also asking one half of one of his classes to write descriptions of methods which could be used by the other half.

The department were not yet at a stage where it was possible to see the outcomes of their language policy work. They were still very much in the middle of it.

Home Economics

Two members of the Home Economics Department at School 3 had taken part in a course on language and learning in Home Economics provided by the local teachers' centre. Their greatest gains from the course were habits of monitoring and questioning their own practices. For instance, there was usually a cassette tape-recorder in the room during their lessons. At some stage in a lesson one group would record its work onto cassette. At first the teachers would review their lessons with the aid of a tape-recording, listening, for example, for closed questions (with one correct reply) which pretend to be open-ended. Later they turned to writing, asking, for instance, 'Am I setting this writing as a genuine learning activity or is it just an exercise?' They realized how easy it is to set writing which is 'really just to cover yourself', to show that your classes are working.

The head of department was well aware that most of her colleagues had not had the advantage of a language and learning course. But there was another problem. A number of the department, experienced and established teachers, had considered themselves cookery teachers, yet curriculum development in Home Economics meant they were being asked, for example, to teach about detergents and 'a little bit of the science of detergency'. Providing books and materials for the new work, and encouraging colleagues to go as often as possible to outside meetings on new Home Economics teaching, became priorities. Members of the department were collecting together new ideas for teaching, either with the emphasis on the development of the Home Economics curriculum, or on language and learning. Inevitably this brought a problem of communication. The department was in the habit of meeting informally in the staffroom to talk briefly about the morning's or afternoon's work. The head of department, therefore, chose to make time-tabled department meetings rather formal, with minutes being taken and a tight time schedule. She felt that this was necessary in a department such as hers which had three or four part-time staff who might well miss the informal break and lunchtime encounters with colleagues. Such staff must feel, if they could get to meetings, that their time was being used profitably and, if they could not, that they were being kept in touch.

Each member of the department, too, had a 'Bullock file'. Having attended the teachers' centre course, and being a member of the school's first language policy committee, the Head of Home Economics well appreciated the time-consuming nature of learning about language and learning. She therefore arranged for the files to contain copies of extracts or reviews, notes on open questions made in response to a department discussion, outlines of the variety of work possible in a particular topic and so on. Members of the department contributed as well. For instance, two staff compiled a list of Fog Index ratings (a measure of 'reading difficulty')[1] for most of the books regularly used in the department. Language and learning had come, therefore, to figure in department discussions and meetings; but what difference did this interest and concern make in lessons? The two members of the department who had attended the teachers' centre course and felt most confident in talking about their work explained that the clearest outcome had been a greater variety of language activity in their lessons.

As with the report on the PE Department, I concentrate in this account on one lesson, a morning on 'detergency'. The girls, second-years, had spent the previous two weeks on the topic, and were now being asked to work in groups to revise and consolidate their knowledge. On the blackboard was a list of words related to the previous week's lessons:

> water, surface tension, detergent, dirt, hard water,
> soap detergent, synthetic detergent.

The class were grouped round the blackboard and were told: 'Between you, try and remember all the things that relate to the words on the blackboard so that you can explain to us what we've done.' The girls left the blackboard and went into groups for this revision work, which had been carefully set up as a group discussion activity.

I tape-recorded one of the groups at work. Two other groups were tape-recording themselves that day. In this classroom a tape-recorder was a very unremarkable classroom prop, rather than a gimmick from the school's special effects department. Talk, particularly small-group talk, had become an interest of this teacher's as a result of her language and learning course. In this case, as on most of the occasions on which I saw the conditions for such talk being established by this teacher, the girls had been given a clearly defined job, but not one which involved getting a 'right' answer. They knew that they might be asked to report back to their classmates. The following exchange took place at the beginning of one group's discussions:

PUPIL I What do we know about water?
VOICE Don't know.
PUPIL I Water's got surface tension.

VOICE Yes.

VOICE And you can get hard and soft.

PUPIL 1 Water won't soak into garments without –

VOICES [*interrupting*] – a detergent.

VOICE It will.

PUPIL 2 It won't, not properly, because the detergent breaks the surface tension.

PUPIL 1 If you notice when you wash your hair – this is a good example because I found this – when you wash your hair water doesn't soak through your hair, you've still got bits that's still dry, haven't you, but as soon as you put one lot of shampoo on your hair will just go automatically wet.

VOICES Yes, won't it?

VOICES Yes.

PUPIL 1 That's what I always find, anyway.

PUPIL 2 That's the same as with materials though, isn't it, because as soon as you put the detergent in the water the surface tension breaks and then the material gets wet, properly wet I mean.

A short extract such as this can raise many questions: the teacher-like role of Pupil 1, for instance, or the issue of the girls who say relatively little. What I find interesting here is the contribution of Pupil 2 insisting that surface tension is the common explanation of shampoo wetting hair and detergent wetting clothes – an important contribution to the talk. Revision here is a shared job, not just of looking over and memorizing notes, but of pooling and making sense of previous work. After the group revision, with most groups making shared written notes, the class was called together for a reporting-back session. A further important aspect of this teacher's work was the opportunity for pupils to have an audience for what they had either discussed or written. Just as the girls were used to working with a tape-recorder, so they were used to the reporting-back sessions in which one or two of the groups would explain their work to others.

On this occasion the group which reported back were clearly less certain about surface tension than the group I had recorded. Surface tension was mentioned, but its connections with detergency were not touched upon. After the report-back the teacher spoke:

TEACHER That's fine. Good. One or two points. First of all, does anyone want to make any comments as to what they said or bits they didn't really understand? Anybody want to chip in? [*A long pause.*] There's just two points. First of all, when you said about the surface tension experiment and you can prove that there is surface tension because a pin or a needle will float on top of the water, what does a detergent do in that experiment so that you explain what we did to prove that the needle then sank?

[*A long pause. A girl answered. The tape-recorder picked up only some of what she said, that a blob of detergent added to the water makes the needle sink.*]

TEACHER Now, how does that show us how a detergent works when we put it in the water that we're going to wash clothes in? Anyone might answer this. Tracey?

TRACEY [*Pupil 1 from the first extract.*] When you put clothes in the water they're not completely wet unless you put detergent in and the water will soak through.

VOICE The detergent, it breaks the surface tension . . . [*pause*]

TEACHER . . . and makes the water settle into the clothes.

I have deliberately written into the transcript the pauses in the discussion. I do so because the pauses did seem to make a space for people to collect their thoughts before talking. The teacher did not rush in to fill a silence; she became genuinely part of an audience. This was not a case of fortunate intuition on her part. In connection with her interest in language policy she had made and listened to tape-recordings of herself conducting small-group or class lessons, noting particularly critically the style and pacing of her own interventions.

After the revision session and report-back a new set of words went up on the blackboard:

mild detergent   heavy-duty detergent   enzyme detergent

TEACHER Over here and at the far end of the room I've put out two identical selections of detergents – in other words, what I've put out here is exactly the same as what I've put out over there. I want half the class to come and have a look at the various packets, read the packets, look at the labels, try and sort out which are mild, heavy-duty, enzyme, and there may be something that doesn't fit into any of those three.

Has the teacher set a piece of home economics work, or a reading exercise? Or, to abandon the dichotomy, is she recognizing that her pupils need time to read and learn home economics? The task was carefully framed to encourage the girls to read critically. They had to sift through the blarney of a detergent packet copy and extract the little information available which was of use. A teacher not working so thoughtfully with language could have had a much easier time providing a list of detergents to fit the three categories.

What may seem a not particularly significant piece of work provided a crop of difficulties. In what follows, the teacher was working with a girl of low ability and tremendous diffidence. With help the girl established that she was looking at a bottle of fabric conditioner, not a detergent. The conditioner was the odd one out in the assembly of detergent packets. But the difficulties then started:

TEACHER Now, it's a fabric conditioner. Now, is that what a detergent is? [*A long pause.*]

JANE Yes.

TEACHER Is it? Isn't it? Oh, what is it? What do you think a fabric con – What does a hair conditioner do?

JANE It keeps your hair in the way you want.

TEACHER It keeps your hair in the way you want it. OK, now, does a detergent do that with clothes?

JANE No.

TEACHER What does it do, then?

JANE Cleans them.

TEACHER Cleans them. So is a fabric conditioner the same as a detergent? [*A long pause.*] Let me just remind you. A fabric conditioner, meaning clothes – that's what fabrics are, clothes – is the same as a hair conditioner, and you've just told me what a hair conditioner – what does it do?

JANE Keeps your hair in place.

TEACHER Keeps your hair in place. So a fabric conditioner does what to clothes?

JANE Keeps them straight?

TEACHER All right, keeps them nice. Looking how they should do. Is that the same as what a detergent does? What does a detergent do? [*A long pause.*] Why do you put clothes in detergent water?

JANE Get the dirt out.

TEACHER Get the dirt out. So do you think that [*indicating the fabric conditioner*] is a detergent?

JANE Yes.

TEACHER You think it is. Now you've made me stuck, because I thought you said to me that a fabric conditioner – Look, a fabric conditioner works like a hair conditioner, yes? If you put a hair conditioner on your hair it would make it go all nice and soft and feel silky and it would stay in the place that you wanted. All right, if you put a fabric conditioner – if I washed this and then I put it in a fabric conditioner it would feel all nice . . .

JANE For making it softer.

TEACHER It's making it softer. Yes. Is it for cleaning it?

JANE No.

TEACHER Because, look, it says here, 'Use for rinsing your whole wash.' It doesn't say, 'Use for washing it.' It says, 'Use for rinsing it.' Do you think, think that is a detergent for getting the dirt out? So should that be on this table with all these other things? Why shouldn't it? You're there.

JANE They all clean the clothes, and that makes them softer.

TEACHER That's right.

The teacher introduced hair conditioner, which Jane was familiar with, either from home or from earlier lessons on skin and hair care. With the teacher's help Jane could then infer from her own description of a hair conditioner that a fabric conditioner would in some way be similar. But she then had great difficulty in separating that description of a conditioner from her description of what a detergent does; she did not recognize the lack of logic in saying that a conditioner softens and that it washes clothes like a detergent. Yet painstakingly the teacher persisted in building up the meaning with Jane of 'conditioner' and 'detergent'. It was a time-consuming way of teaching, building and checking understanding in talk rather than simple telling by the teacher. Yet the lesson was organized in such a way as to make this possible, with groups working busily at their tasks and the teacher freed to give attention to individuals.

The job of sorting out detergents had been quite a difficult one for a number of girls and so the teacher asked them, in the next part of the lesson, to explain 'in your own words' how they had done the sorting. The teacher found one girl, Kate, who had quickly got into a muddle. She had written: 'Lux is a soap flake which is a minimum weight.' The teacher told Kate what minimum weight meant: 'It's telling you how much soap there is in that packet,' and then asked her to read the description of Lux from the packet. Kate hesitated over the word 'delicate'. Everything else she read accurately, though rather slowly.

TEACHER Now, does that tell you anything about Lux and whether it's a mild detergent in the way it handles your clothes or a heavy-duty one and it'll be harsher on your clothes?
KATE This one's soft.
TEACHER It's soft. So it's a mild detergent. Now, you read through what you've written down there. Is that what you've put? 'Lux is a soap flake which is a minimum weight.'
  [Kate reads her writing.]
Well, what does that mean? I don't know what that means.
  [Kate's reply is inaudible.]
So it's on the box here. Why have you written that down? Did you understand what that meant? Really minimum weight is telling you how much soap there is in that box, how much you're buying. Now does that have anything to do with its being a mild detergent?
KATE No.
TEACHER Do you think that that bit there does? Yes. So what we're trying to say is that if it's a mild detergent you can wash delicate or, as they tell you, pretty blouses and night wear and underwear, fine things that you want to keep because it won't harm them. It tells you everything you wash by hand is safer and softer with Lux. That's your mild detergent, you're not going to get big dirty greasy stains off. All right.

Again the teacher intervened to help the pupil build up sense and understanding, reading aloud herself and showing how *she* was reading the detergent packet to make sense of what she had asked the girls to do. We may not be able to *teach* pupils how to read comprehendingly but we can give them something of the experience by sharing it with them.

At this stage in her language policy work, the head of department was still concerned to involve more of her staff, and was puzzling how best to do this. She was concerned, too, about writing in her subject. She was beginning to ask what would be the best ways of introducing pupils to the full essay-writing which would be required of them in examination work. Yet, when we looked back on lessons, it seemed that the problem was half answered: she could set up essay-planning as a small-group talk and report activity, thus building on the work that had so far come out of her commitment to language work.

History

The History Department at School 3 had also benefited because one of its members had worked directly with the curriculum development project director from the local teachers' centre. Another member of the department was a member of one of the school's language policy groups. Inevitably, and appropriately, the changes language policy work had brought had come in gradually and in selected areas of the syllabus. We chose the second-year work as an area to look at because the head of department had devised a new course for that year group, based on the *What is History?* kit from the Schools Council 13–16 History Project.[2] I report below on lessons from that course.

The head of department was explicit about the connections between the syllabus changes she had made and language. 'If you reshape history you have to reshape the language,' she said. History as she had previously thought of it and taught it involved taking a familiar journey from the Romans in the first year, 'along the conveyor belt of knowledge', to modern times. The emphasis now was on fewer topics done in greater detail, each topic designed to offer pupils a variety of language activity: interviews, trial speeches, conversations and so on. So far, this may sound like little more than a sophisticated version of the 'day in the life of' style of history which most of us in our own schooldays were probably allowed to do occasionally as leavening in the usual flat fare of notes and essays. But here it had a more thoughtful place in the department's work. For instance, the department had always tried to use some documentary evidence with pupils, but had found them unable to differentiate textbook material from original evidence. Furthermore, it seemed that pupils tended to take everything they read in a textbook as 'gospel truth' and would sometimes react to topics quite subjectively and uncritically. In other words, even though most of the pupils coming to history lessons could read, very few of them knew how to read to learn and understand history.

The availability of reading materials in history, as in all school subjects with the exception of English, presents great problems. Primary sources are difficult because they are often written in a language which only specialist historians would not find taxing. School textbooks can also be difficult, and the new textbooks, glossily and colourfully produced, often contain more difficult language than the old-fashioned-looking books with faded green and brown covers which are still available in many schools. The History Department at School 3 found that their pupils often used the old textbooks effectively, simply because they were well-indexed and organized in such a way that pupils could find their way around them.

As with the Home Economics Department, the main result of rethinking the curriculum had been to offer pupils a greater variety of talking, reading and writing activities, particularly in the lower school. The Head of History felt especially regretful that, because of the constraints of the examination syllabus, she was still teaching much more traditionally in the upper school. 'We never finish the syllabus anyway,' she told me, so she had decided to reconsider her examination work. The work she had so far done with an O-level class included a prediction exercise: the girls formulated a blueprint for a dictatorship, having read about and discussed the rise of Hitler and Mussolini. The same group of O-level students took part in a simulation game of a summit conference. However, this teacher was aware that such activities were still excursions from the traditional style of examination-syllabus history teaching.

More recently a member of the department, who was also on one of the school's language policy committees, had explored with that committee the topic of writing. Each committee member took one of his or her teaching groups and made available a wider choice of writing topics than was usually presented. The committee then wrote up and, in conjunction with the teachers' centre, published accounts of what they had done. Members of the history teacher's lower-sixth A-level group were asked: 'Set out a piece of writing on the Constitutional Crisis of 1909–11. This is not to be in continuous prose or note form.' Three of the pupils who did the work subsequently made a tape-recording, reflecting on what they had done. One of them had chosen to write in diagrammatic form, another imaginatively, as a peer living at the time of the crisis, and a third had produced work representing a series of newspaper clippings. What came out of their transcribed report was the way in which their choices had made them take up issues of evidence and bias.

Not all members of the department were so interested in the school's language policy work as the two I have mentioned, and some expressed concern that some of the new ways of working introduced into the department made it difficult to assess children and keep track of their progress as before. With this problem in mind, the head of department had included the second-year history syllabus in the Curriculum Development Committee's work on assessment (see p. 102 above).

The class I watched was a second-year mixed-ability group working on the second of the mysteries presented in the *What is History?* unit. Pupils are given a modern mystery and then a historical mystery to solve. The idea is that they will learn that the historian has much in common with the detective. He or she must work at interpreting evidence, must appreciate the difference between fact and speculation, and must often be content to provide the likeliest explanation rather than a certain one. The first mystery, which the class had already investigated, involved dealing with evidence to explain the death of Mark Pullen, whose body had been found dumped on a roadside. Clues, which could serve as evidence, were gradually supplied, forcing the pupils to modify their initial surmises. The second mystery was also a death, the death of Tollund Man, but unlike the Mark Pullen case this had happened long ago. To start off, the class were given their first pieces of information. They were shown a series of slides of Tollund Fen and of the body that was uncovered by two peat-cutters. Each slide, indeed each item introduced, gave more possible evidence about the death but imposed more constraints on one's speculations.

The Schools Council pamphlet describes the body:

On his head he wore a pointed skin cap fastened securely under the chin by a hide thong. Round his waist there was a smooth hide belt. Otherwise he was naked. His hair was cropped so short as to be almost entirely hidden by his cap. He was clean-shaven but there was very short stubble on the chin and upper lip ... Underneath [his head] was a rope, made of two leather thongs twisted together. This was a noose. It was drawn tight around his neck and throat and then coiled like a snake over his shoulder and down across his back.

Having seen these details on slide the class were asked to turn to their report sheets (reproduced here on p. 126) to see just how much they could fill in. The activity proved to be an interesting one, as the following transcript shows:

THINGS TO FIND OUT

1. Who found the body?
2. Where was the body found?
3. What clothing or possessions were found on or near the body?
4. What was the age of the man?
5. How long had he been dead?
6. Which of the following was the most likely cause of death?

Old Age	Yes/No
	Explanation for your answer.
Disease	Yes/No
	Explanation for your answer.
Suicide	Yes/No
	Explanation for your answer.
Murder	Yes/No
	Explanation for your answer.

7. Reason for death (why did he die in this way?)
   Your theory:

   Supporting evidence:

8. Conclusions and comments:

Signed: ....

TEACHER Right, question four: What age was the man? How many people managed to answer this one?
PUPIL I He was very old.
TEACHER How do you know he was very old?
PUPIL I Because his face was all wrinkled.
TEACHER But is that a sign of age? I know a lot of young people who've got horrible wrinkled faces.
PUPIL I But he didn't look – he looked old.
TEACHER He looked old. If people look old they've got to be old.
PUPIL 2 Well, he was old when they found him.
PUPIL 3 Thirty-six.

TEACHER Thirty-six! My goodness, you are accurate. How did you know he was thirty-six?
PUPIL 3 I didn't. I just guessed.

Many pupils had provided answers for the rest of the questions. One girl said that the man had not been long dead because his body had not gone mouldy, a very soundly based answer. Less well based was a claim that the cause of death was murder. Several felt that the man could not have died of a disease because he had no signs of disease on his body. Generally, there had been a scrabble to provide answers to all the questions. The teacher reminded the class of the Mark Pullen case and of how many had guessed their 'solutions' to the mystery of his death. She reminded them how they had had to review their ideas as new evidence had been given to them. For the next stage of the lesson the teacher read to the class the scientific report on the body from the fen, which indicated the date of the burial (about 2000 years ago). The report also supplied information about the last meal eaten by the man (a soup of vegetables and spring seeds – probably a special meal). It was inconclusive about the cause of the man's death but it did rule out disease and head injury. Although a noose was round the man's neck, the report said that there was no conclusive evidence that this had been the cause of his death. Furnished with this scientific explanation, the class again worked in groups on the answers to their report sheet, and in a further question-and-answer session established that they could now answer all the report sheet questions except why the man had died. Around this topic there were one or two bits of interesting speculation: If the man had not eaten for almost twenty-four hours before he died, surely his death was planned? Did the special food in his gut indicate that he had been sacrificed (this a speculation from Debbie)? If the noose was not necessarily responsible for his death, perhaps it was a sign that the man was a slave, but then if he was a slave why had he eaten special food (the remains of the soup found in the gut contained several rare items)? I was beginning to appreciate what the Head of History had meant by reshaping the history and so reshaping the language. The discussion seemed to indicate that the girls were learning to respect evidence.

In the following lesson I was able to tape one of the groups at work. The lesson opened with a further quick showing of the slides, another reading of the scientific report, and the final material, 'Some clues about the life and customs of the Iron Age people': two extracts from Cornelius Tacitus, a Roman commentator on the Germanic tribes of Denmark, and information about two similar bodies found in the Danish Fens. The material to be used to answer the questions on the report sheet was difficult, so the teacher provided a set of her own questions on the blackboard to help the girls assess their evidence:

1. List the different reasons why Tollund Man may have been killed.
2. What have the three bodies found in common?
3. What have only *two* got in common?
4. Can you think of any reason why the rope was found round their neck other than because it killed them?

There was a longer session for group talk this time as the groups had to come up with a theory about the death of Tollund Man. The four girls I taped pieced together what the bodies had in common: the meal of spring seeds; the fact that all of them had been found in a bog; all had something wrong with their neck. How the man died still presented problems; there were too many possibilities. For instance, they puzzled, if the man had drowned in the bog why was there a noose around his neck? Perhaps, one of them suggested, he might have been pulled along by it. But another member of the group pointed out that Tollund Man's neck was not marked. Yet another member had a different idea:

MANDY Oh, you know they have everybody or everybody has a noose on, right, with a loop in it.
DEBBIE Mm?
MANDY You ever seen 'em on telly?
DEBBIE Yes, they have a rope on each one.
MANDY That's right, they all link up and all walk along.
PUPIL 3 That's a good idea.
MANDY Like, er, that's it, right, that's the man's body, right, and it's round his neck and there's a big loop there and it joins up all of them.
PUPIL 3 Chuck 'em in.
MANDY That's probably the connection.
DAWN So they wouldn't run away when they were washing the chariot. [*It had been suggested that the men were slaves serving the Spring Goddess and washing her chariot.*]
MANDY Yes, but why were they naked?

Mandy's contribution here with its reference to telly programmes may at first seem to have little to do with Tollund Man. But in fact she did use her memory of TV programmes to try out an explanation that would fit: if the noose was not responsible for death by strangulation (and there was no sign that it was), what could it have been used for? She also reminded her friends of the piece of information that didn't fit: all the bodies found were naked. Subsequently, they considered whether or not any clothing worn by the men would have rotted away in the 2000 years of burial and decided that if the neck ropes and leather caps had not rotted, neither, probably, would clothing.

Mandy went on to explain to her friends her theory that a good master had an ungrateful slave who stole and was killed for his crimes. But generally – and very impressively – the conversation kept more closely to the evidence: If the men were sacrifices, why were slaves sacrificed? Why were they fed unusual food before death? Why should one of the men have a birch branch across his body? It wasn't used to beat him to death because there were no marks. Interestingly, it was Mandy who kept a good overall sense of where the talk was going and what was still unresolved.

MANDY There's only one man who's confusing and that's the man who had the branch on him and that's the same man who had his ears cut to here, that's the same man.

What she wasn't doing at this stage was to see the mismatch between her respect for the detail of the evidence and her overall rather wild theory. When the group came to write out their shared ideas she asked to discuss 'as we go along', admitting that she was still confused.

Connected with the Tollund Man mystery was work on primary and secondary sources in historical data. In a group discussion session a class worked out what kinds of materials a biographer could get together to investigate their own lives. Another second-year class who had just finished studying Tollund Man went on to look at a series of slides on classical Greece. The slide lesson was held for two classes at once. The large size of the group and limited time almost dictated a fairly rapid general question-and-answer session. The idea of the session was to encourage pupils to look at things from the past, in this case slides of articles from classical Greece, and to begin to appreciate them as sources of information. Thus what one pupil guessed to be a wine jar because 'it looks tablish' could tell something about craftsmanship, crops and climate. Subsequently, in groups, the pupils chose photographs of the slides to study in greater detail to consider what they could reveal and (just as important) what questions they suggested. A small group looking at a picture of the Parthenon were alerted to ask about building materials, Greek writing and religion, and could turn to the books and material available – collected together from the history stock rooms and school library. The exercise of going to textbooks with their own questions was an important part of their training. A group I taped came across references to the *Odyssey*. The expression, 'their hearts were full of wondering', which one of them read out, alerted her to suggest that this was 'writing for interest and entertainment, not just facts'.

Like the Humanities Department in School 1, the History Department here were collecting together as many primary sources as they could. They had established co-operation with the local museum, and during my stay at the school a representative from the museum came along, with a case full of artifacts, to talk about life in a nearby town during the time of the Industrial Revolution. The talk was for third-years who amongst their work on the period were studying factory conditions with the aid of evidence taken by the Factory Commission of 1833.

As in School 1, interest in classroom language had led to a greater emphasis on small-group talk, which was one feature of the new work some members of the department felt it was particularly difficult to assess. The department were also beginning to encourage different kinds of writing, not because they wanted variety for variety's sake, but because the traditional notes or essays were often no longer an appropriate part of the new methods.

What they had not yet done was to make tape-recordings of themselves at work with classes or groups of children. Other teachers in the school, in Science, in Home Economics and in PE, for instance, had done this, in the course of their enquiries into language, and I have indicated some of the questions that occurred as a result. It enabled these teachers both to listen critically to their own questions, interjections and instructions, and to follow the process of learning some of their pupils' talk. The Head of History did realize that she probably talked a great deal in lessons (too much, according to the survey made by the Language Policy Committee!), but she had not yet realized that that might be impeding the investigations that she was encouraging the children to make.

Summary

Looking over language policy work at School 3 I see these as its key features:

1 The work had been incorporated into the body of the school through
   a the Language Policy Committee's liaison with the Curriculum Working Party and Consultative Committee;
   b the surveys which were the outcomes of these liaisons; and
   c the allocation, wherever possible, of extra time to Language Policy Committee members to pursue the work.
2 In spite of uncertainties, the original Language Policy Committee managed to create interest across the curriculum, presenting

language as a school-wide issue, and yet found ways of working in detail by examining and modifying classroom practice.

3 Alongside the work going on in the school went support from the curriculum development project of the local teachers' centre.

I have mentioned the work of the curriculum development project director. It is not possible to give details of all of the work at the centre from which teachers at the school have benefited, but it included the following features:

1 Courses on language and learning for particular subject areas were available. For example, two teachers from the Home Economics Department attended a course which dealt with
   a language acquisition;
   b the Bullock recommendations in the light of their own teaching;
   c an examination of their training at college; and
   d consideration and analysis of tapes made by teachers on the course in their own classrooms.

2 A group of teachers were meeting regularly at the centre, and at the time of my visit were considering language in science and bringing along tapes and transcripts of themselves at work.

3 A series of meetings on reading and reading development for two local secondary schools (one of them School 3) was in progress.

4 The project director was co-ordinating all the work done in the local authority's schools, and producing language packs. A language pack is a folder of material on language and learning produced in local schools (plus a few items of interest from elsewhere). The teaching survey and homework survey were among School 3's contribution to the packs.

5 The project director, apart from attending committee meetings, had been into lessons in various departments in the school – P E, Science, History, Home Economics – and discussed those lessons with the teachers concerned.

6 A day conference on language across the curriculum had been organized with delegates from many local schools. Four members from School 3 attended. Delegates shared ideas and problems and produced a discussion document.

It isn't possible to assess how much of the work done by the language policy committees at the school was a result of the support given by the teachers' centre. Reciprocating that support was the readiness of teachers to attend courses and meetings and spend much more time on language work than the two extra periods allowed from the timetable. What was important, too, was the recognition by the head of the school of the significance of *A Language for Life* and the way in which she established language work and provided the first group with resources to work as a functioning committee in the school.

The courses run at the centre may help to explain why language policy work at the school could move from the initial school survey work to considerations of classroom practice. The Head of Home Economics and the Head of Science had both attended courses on language and learning in their subjects at the centre and had met teachers from other schools.

In contrast was the approach of the Head of PE, who, with a little consultation with the curriculum project director, evolved her own framework for looking at language in PE lessons. She acknowledged that she was motivated to do her work because of the enthusiasm of the Language Policy Committee and the support and interest she could call upon from 'Bullock' colleagues.

The enthusiasm itself came not only from the excitement of learning together that these teachers experienced but from the support expressed by the head in following the Bullock Report's Recommendation 139 and embodying their work in the organizational structure of the school.

References

1. See, for example, Eric Lunzer and Keith Gardner, *The Effective Use of Reading*, Heinemann Educational for the Schools Council, 1979, pp. 76–9 and 91–6.
2. The materials used from this kit included: the teacher's guide and filmstrip notes; Unit 2a, 'Detective Work: The Mystery of Mark Pullen' (wallet); Unit 2b, 'Detective Work: The Mystery of Tollund Man' (leaflet, slides, spiritmaster report sheet); and Unit 3a, 'Looking at Evidence: How do we know about Classical Greece?' (filmstrip). All were published for the Schools Council by Holmes McDougall, Edinburgh, 1976.

V. Case study 4

School 4 is a mixed school in London, with eight-form entry in a normal year, and is a genuine neighbourhood school in a way that few in London are. This is largely because the school is in, or rather part of, a fairly cohesive old-fashioned working-class neighbourhood, preserving its identity in spite of the decline of dock work and printing, the two representative industries, and in spite of redevelopment by the local council, which tore down old terraces and replaced them with blocks connected by walkways and skirted by roads. The area is still much 'whiter' than are many places near to it. There are some West Indian, Cypriot and Asian children in the school, the majority of whom come across as Londoners. The West Indian group, which is probably the most sizeable, does not identify itself as an alternative culture in the way that some such groups in London schools do. Recently, in response to ILEA policy, the school set up a working party to look at race relations and at the threat of racism presented by groups such as the National Front.

The school is on two sites, about twelve minutes' walk apart. The lower school is a nineteenth-century three-decker building which houses first- and second-years. The upper school is an odd collection of buildings, a jumble of sizes and styles skirted on two sides by a very busy, noisy street feeding into a main trunk road.

At age 11, ILEA children are grouped in three broad bands of ability, band one being the top. The school used to have an intake largely of 'twos' and 'threes', but authority intervention has meant a significant increase of band one children. For a large number of parents in the neighbourhood the school is the first choice. First- and second-years work largely in mixed-ability groups. In the third year there is setting (grouping by ability) for mathematics and languages. In the fourth year options begin, with English the only subject continuing with mixed-ability tutor groups.

Language work

Language policy work at the school pre-dates the Bullock Report and arose initially from a staff conference in 1973. Originally intended as a day's meeting to consider the fourth- and fifth-year curriculum, the conference turned its attention to what it felt was a more urgent underlying problem, basic reading and writing in the first three years of the school. As a result a working group of volunteers, supported by the staff, was formed. The group was made up of a teacher of remedial reading, the leader of the World Studies team in the lower school, the Head of English and the Director of Studies (a modern linguist in overall charge of curriculum and timetabling). The group's brief was not specified in detail.

In this first stage of the school's language policy work the working group was concerned to involve as many staff as possible on the lower school site in basic problems of reading and writing, regardless of subject specialisms. It was decided that the best way to do this was probably to encourage work with tutor groups and to concentrate on handwriting. Two members of staff produced an A4 pamphlet, *Start Write*, 'a course for correcting faults in printed script', and *Write On*, 'a course in cursive handwriting based on simple modern hand'. These carefully produced pamphlets have had wide success outside the school and have been sold to other London schools. The course needs to be taught sensitively so that children appreciate that they are being asked to be careful, neat and precise. Otherwise it could become a tutor period time-filler where pupils simply rush through the exercises. But, with this proviso, the handwriting course can be an effective way of alerting teachers to difficulties, and of providing immediate remedial help.

A second part of the basic language work was more ambitious, and nearer to the central concerns of language and learning, because it focused on the process rather than the output of language use. The working group wanted to deal with a topic wide enough to involve many staff and this time chose the writing of worksheets. They advised that worksheets should be written so that children had to answer in sentences, and should be marked with emphasis on sentence structure as well as on content. The scheme failed to involve Departments as had been hoped, partly because these were the days of high staff turnover and there was no one with a specific responsibility for briefing new staff. Moreover, there was no time officially devoted to language and learning when teachers could get together and monitor what they were doing.

As the scheme included moves towards making the language issue broad enough to be applicable to and of interest to almost everyone, it was also closely concerned with changing teaching practices. Experience from other schools in this series of case studies suggests that a language policy committee can work effectively across the curriculum if it is given the time and a brief to 'research' and report back on particular issues. It is unrealistic to think that such committees can have a say in how reports will be taken up in departments. A committee can pose questions, open up problems and offer more or less compelling evidence. But it is unlikely to directly affect practices in an individual department, which is what the worksheet recommendations had set out to do, without support for its general direction and effective communication with subject specialists.

The third aspect of stage one of the school's language work, and one which developed to become the lower school's official language policy, was a basic literacy programme (see pp. 139–142 below for details). The Head of World Studies (an integrated course for the first and second years, covering English, history and geography) agreed to give over a double period per group per week to enable all the children, except those considered very able, to do the basic literacy programme. Half a year group at a time (about 120 children) joined the literacy scheme in an effort to make five teachers available plus, if at all possible, a parent or sixth-former. Several sixth-formers regularly helped, but involving parents proved as difficult in this working-class London area as it did in the middle-class environs of School 1, despite the fact that two open meetings were held each year so that parents could be told about the literacy schemes. There were usually also three remedial teachers available in literacy time blocked for each half-year group, to give the detailed tuition that some children needed. An advanced literacy scheme, for more able children in years one and two, included detailed studies of poetry or novels, story-writing techniques and some 'straightforward English grammar'. The scheme was described by the Head of English as 'some of the things that one would expect to happen in ordinary English lessons', but which did not always happen here because English was part of World Studies.

Fourth- and fifth-year pupils in need of extra help with reading presented particular problems. Special provision was made for them at the time that the lower-school literacy scheme was being developed. The difficulty was withdrawing them from lessons, which an adequate reading programme required, and at the same time expecting them to pursue a full syllabus leading to examinations. The working group suggested that extra English should be offered as a normal subject option with a teacher to pupil ratio of 1:10, a considerable drain on staffing and funding. Since this option was first offered, each year approximately sixty fifth-year pupils and over sixty fourth-year pupils chose to reduce their number of examination courses in order to concentrate on extra English work.

Perhaps the most serious danger in a literacy scheme, with literacy being regarded as a 'subject', is that it may bear no relation to a child's experiences in the rest of his or her timetable. At School 4 the staff involved with the literacy scheme were the World Studies teachers who took the same group of pupils in their literacy class for a further eight periods of their working week, and so at least knew what they had achieved in the scheme. What remained uncertain was how to use knowledge of a child's performance on a work book to guide understanding of his or her linguistic capabilities when he or she was doing ordinary lessons. This applied in particular to the main 'reading workshop' component of the scheme (discussed more comprehensively on pp. 139–143).

Although one may consider the view of language and learning involved in devising the literacy and reading schemes as oriented too much towards desired standards ('core abilities') rather than how such standards are achieved by a variety of purposive ways of using language, one needs to remember that the schemes pre-date the Bullock Report and the extensive debates on language and learning that followed its publication. One needs to appreciate, too, the help in implementing the literacy schemes given by the Director of Studies, who could implement the recommendations of the working group (of which he was a member) as a curriculum matter. Representation on a school's language policy committee by whoever is responsible for managing the curriculum (as in Schools 1, 2 and 4) or direct access to that person or body (as at School 3) is critical. Indeed without it one can say that language policy work is not being taken seriously and will fail to become established as part of the school's everyday life.

THE LANGUAGE POLICY DOCUMENT

The second stage of language work at the school led to the production of its language policy document. Shortly after the publication of the Bullock Report the ILEA requested (in a strongly worded circular that could not easily be ignored) that all its schools, primary and secondary, should produce a language policy statement. The Director of Studies chaired the meeting at which the value of compiling such a document was discussed. He suggested to the staff that they could produce a paper written as a response to a bureaucratic request as a way of keeping County Hall quiet and as a public relations exercise, or they could write a more honest document. The teachers, many of whom had a pride in the conscientiousness and quality of their work and a sense of being part of a good staff, decided to take the request seriously and carry out a survey of how language was being regarded and used over the range of subjects. These findings would then be described, and connections between subjects and practices made. This was to form the basis for making recommendations for change. The survey and the recommendations would be written as the formal policy document.

The group who had been responsible for setting up the lower-school literacy programme devised a questionnaire to be studied and answered by all departments. The group analysed replies and used them as had been suggested. The document they produced had the following sections:

1. Intentions (a résumé of the group's interpretation of their brief)
2. Environment (community and intake)
3. Pupil patterns (a breakdown of subject time available for the first three years, fourth- and fifth-year options, and the sixth form)
4. Curriculum
5. Terminology definitions
6. Basic skills: the literacy scheme
7. Correction and marking
8. The role of the English and Remedial Departments
9. Reading
10. Writing
11. Talking
12. Conclusion.

The reading section is reproduced in Appendix C to give an impression of the document as a whole. It is full of references to current practice which inform the recommendations it makes. Many teachers thinking about the reading of their pupils for the first time would probably find it educative as it sketches out what is still to be done rather than concentrating on descriptions of what had been achieved.

The document was presented to the school at a meeting at the end of 1976, four years after the previous day conference which launched the literacy scheme. The staff asked for another such conference at which they could form working groups (a mixture of departments) to look at different parts of the policy. When this was eventually held in May 1977, it was generally felt to be a disappointment. The document was, in some ways, too successful. It stated clearly and persuasively the nature of the problem, served to introduce language across the curriculum concerns to the uninitiated and made a number of very manageable recommendations. The work now had to be done in departments, in classrooms. The practicalities of how that might go ahead were of more pressing interest than a further rehearsal of general issues. The group who had compiled the document had neither the time nor the expertise to do this detailed guiding of colleagues from all areas of the curriculum. Some months after the day conference, realizing the problem that they had come up against, the four people who edited the language policy document produced a statement for the school's Academic Committee (see Appendix D). One outcome of this was the setting up of a new policy committee on language. Each department was to select a representative, preferably, it was felt, a young member of the department, making in all a committee of fifteen. Individual members were to be responsible for reporting back to their departments.

It seemed at first that the new committee, which began meeting in spring 1978, was going to re-work old ground and come up against old problems. They revived the idea of key-word lists, which had been a secondary element in the literacy scheme, as a way of establishing pupils' competence with a 'common-core' vocabulary of about 400 basic words. The list that had been generally used comprised '100 words which make up, on average, half of all reading' plus another 315 which were 'used to complete the basic sight vocabularies of E. W. Dolch, J. McNally, W. Murray and the Ladybird Keywords, together with words denoting relationships of space, time, number and conditions, colours, months of the year and days of the week, and letters of the alphabet'. All teachers were asked to help children to spell, understand and use these words and add to the list any they thought had the same vital role in their own subjects. Lists of key words, however, do not really engage problems of language and learning because just putting them up and recommending their use neglects the issue of exactly what is to be done with them. Before such a decision is made there needs to be a consideration of the place and appropriateness of specialist language, of the intricacies of engaging with a child's own experience of language as a resource by which he or she will come to new language uses and new understanding. This can only be done by examining one's own practice. The lists in School 4 had, in fact, done little more than decorate walls. The committee probably sensed the lack of progress on this front, for nothing much more was heard of key words, and they went on instead to discuss the processes of taking notes from talks and making notes from texts.

As with the committee in School 1, which was selected on lines similar to this one, much will depend on the goodwill of departments and con-scientiousness of their representatives and on whether someone emerges who can give the committee effective guidance in developing a radical reassessment of existing practices, without which discussions of, say, note-making may just end up rationalizing and sanctioning patterns of work already established.

The literacy scheme

An important element in the lower-school language policy was the liter-acy scheme, the origins of which have been described in the introductory section on the school's language work. Literacy time had been taken out of World Studies time and occupied two periods per week. A half-year group was timetabled to do literacy at the same time. The lessons were run by the classes' regular World Studies teachers with as much help from elsewhere as could be mustered (see p. 135 above). The key item in the basic literacy scheme was the Ward Lock Reading Workshop Scheme, initially chosen because it could be used by children without the assistance of a specialist reading teacher. After the autumn half-term in their first year, some pupils were selected to go to advanced literacy groups. These ran during normal literacy time and usually there would be two groups of about eight children from each half-year, working on imaginative writing, further reading, more grammar, learning to use the library and discussing magazines or their current reading.

As the pros and cons of reading schemes are a matter of current debate, it seems worth while to indicate what I found to be the merits and failings of this particular kit. First of all, of course, such a scheme cannot be claimed as a response to the language needs of individual children. True, each child is tested to see at which step he or she should take up the scheme, but this is simply a need of the scheme rather than of the child. One of the tasks the children have to perform, once they have read a passage, is to find in that passage words which mean the same as a word or phrase given on their question sheet. For example, they are asked to find a word that means moving to and fro (waving); fenced-off areas (corrals); putting your feet down (stepping). Because the scheme can allow only one answer it necessarily precludes other possib-ilities, including those of the child. One example of this difficulty, among many, was provided by a first-year girl who could not work out a word meaning the same as a little river. In the text were mentioned 'stream' and 'lake' which she knew referred to water, but, as I learned by talking to her, in her scheme of things a stream was not the same as a little river. A stream to her was much smaller and, possibly, eventually ran into a river. 'Little river' would not fit as her answer. But 'lake' did not seem right either, except that it was the only other kind of water mentioned. It was at this stage that she came for help. Reading kits such as this have to assume that a pupil's interpretation of potential synonyms will be the same as that decided on beforehand by the kit's author. They cannot recognize individual differences or the relevance of personal contexts, which may allow a child to use the words appropriately and communicatively but not in the prescribed way. In the instance I have just cited, such a context means trouble for the scheme and uncertainty for the child.

The passages which form the basis of the reading work would strike most English teachers as tedious if not impoverished. I think it fair to say that they did not seem to strike most of the children I saw at work in this way. They seemed to appeal to the collector's instinct of a good number of children who enjoyed finding out this and that (many of them I asked seemed to think that the Ward Lock scheme was about 'giving you knowledge – things you don't know about', rather than about reading). Of course, as the children became more familiar with the scheme they grew used to its way of working and adept at short-cutting it. They scanned for the words which seemed to fit questions rather than reading thoroughly. Again this seems an inevitable outcome of such a scheme. Because it works to a formula children will develop formulae to deal with it. There is some evidence to suggest that reading schemes do lead to general reading improvement as measured by a reading-age test, but this is a recommendation which has to be considered alongside the drawbacks I have described. And one has to remember that many reading-age scores reflect only one kind of reading, recognition of isolated words, rather than understanding of passages read as a whole.

The 'non-advanced' children who came through the Ward Lock scheme were then put into a variety of follow-up work such as dictionary exercises, none of which was felt by the teachers to be particularly suitable. At an end-of-year review meeting of the literacy scheme in July 1978 there was general agreement among the staff concerned that a comprehensive reading scheme of 'real books' should be found to cater for these pupils' further development.

The advanced literacy groups were run in parallel with the mainstream classes. The aim of their course, to quote from a statement by the head of English, was 'to use the ability of good readers to open up fairly sophisticated avenues of English/language work, and to equip them for more advanced work in the future'. About half of advanced literacy time was spent on specially devised units of work. There were at the time of my visit units on myths, lyric poetry, ballads, limericks and epitaphs. Some of the units lasted for three or four sessions (each session a double period), some for six or seven sessions (a full half-term's worth of literacy). All of them had been prepared by the English Department (most of them, indeed, by the Head of English). This happened because the lower-school World Studies teachers were occupied, during advanced literacy periods, with the basic course. Teachers from the upper school – where the traditional separation between English, History and Geography Departments is in force – were brought in as visitors to run the advanced course. As a result of their difficulties in travelling over, there was little time for the informal contact and teamwork which might have made materials and teaching more cohesive.

Writing about advanced literacy is much more difficult than writing about the reading scheme because the units (usually collections of material with introduction and explanation) allowed for a much greater variety of teaching styles, as one might expect. The work did give opportunities for shared close and critical reading of a variety of writing and the making and conceding of interpretations, and could lead to, for example, noisy renderings of bawdy limericks. This might well set the scene for writing by the children exploring for themselves the possibilities of, say, a lyric mode. When the units went well they seemed to be much more in harmony with the spirit of Bullock than the basic course. They offered the children a far richer experience of reading, not only because what they read was witty or moving, but also because interpreting meaning, far from being troublesome as in the case of the reading scheme, became the very life of the lesson.

AN EXTERNAL ASSESSMENT

In 1975 a team of analysts from the ILEA's Research and Statistics Branch evaluated the literacy scheme and measured progress using SRA reading test scores, taking three similar schools in London without literacy schemes as controls. It found School 4 pupils did slightly better in terms of reading-test scores than the three control schools and that the difference, although not great, was better than expected by chance. However, the report went on to point out that School 4 had a relatively high proportion of poor readers and that in all schools these were the ones who had made most progress over time. This might partly account for School 4's overall success.

Reading-age scores had improved, then, but not as significantly as might have been expected. The report was rightly reticent about accounting for this, but did point out that staff (apart from the World Studies team) who were asked to display lists of key words and ensure that the children could use and understand them showed 'no great effort or enthusiasm'. The report went on: 'This may have been partly due, as the researcher was told, to the natural inclination of some specialist teachers to see themselves as just that – specialist teachers . . . teaching their particular expertise; *not* as teachers of reading and writing. Another reason, again stressed by some members of staff, may have been the apparent lack of coordination between the different departments in areas such as the "special words" scheme, where coordination would have been of great benefit.'

The reading programme

Another element of language work in the lower school was the reading programme of the Remedial Department. This was a separate department with its own head, working in very close touch with the World Studies Department. Over the previous few years the organization of the Remedial Department had been very thoughtfully and skilfully shaped. Work began in the summer term before a new intake arrived at the school, when the head of department or possibly the head of the new first year visited feeder primary schools and explained to fourth-year juniors that their new secondary school did make provision for non-readers. Anyone who has worked sympathetically with first-years in secondary schools and/or top juniors, allowing them to express their anxieties, will appreciate the fear that a lot of children experience at the prospect of arriving at secondary school unable to read. The Remedial Department was able to gather information about the children who would need attention on these visits by working with a home/school liaison teacher who spent two days per week in School 4 and two days in its main feeder primaries. Co-operation with feeder primary schools is a controversial issue. Some secondary schools feel that they cannot trust their feeder primaries and that learning about their new intake from them can only be the passing on of prejudice. School 4 was particularly fortunate in having a home/school liaison teacher who spent time in some of its local primary schools, and in having a Head of Remedial who set out to get real information.

All the first-year intake was tested. The school had formerly used a Schonell test, at the time of my visit was using a GAP test and planned eventually to use only the new ILEA reading test devised by the authority's Research and Statistics Branch in consultation with teachers. The test produced a raw score which served the purpose of alerting the department to children with great difficulties who could then be given individual diagnostic tests. Current policy was that all children with a reading age of less than 9 years in the first year were withdrawn from ordinary lessons for two periods per week and sent to a reading room instead. There is nothing too significant about reading age 9; it simply provided the department with the numbers it could cope with. It is important to realize that a reading age is a statistical artefact which relies on data gathered in an examination-type situation and that we can expect children to read better in a sympathetic environment than a test might indicate. Working with small groups (ideally of four or five), the reading teacher at School 4 could listen attentively, teach sounds and sound blends when appropriate and, above all, build up the child's confidence.

The department had several reading schemes and shelves of books, all of which were in use. There was probably no one scheme taught exactly as it was originally intended to be. Flexibility and variety were thought to matter more both for pupils and for the teacher. Children would often read into a tape-recorder and then listen to themselves because the head of department considered that she and the child could only know if the child was making sense if he or she was reading aloud. The child could only properly hear himself or herself reading aloud if the reading was on tape. The very poorest readers continued with this type of reading during the basic literacy sessions, to which, wherever possible, the child's reading teacher came along.

The close attention to reading which was given in the Remedial Department (and in advanced literacy) gave children the opportunity to make sure of and check on their understanding of what they were reading. It was much more fluid but less easily monitored than the reading kit used in mainstream literacy classes. It was regrettable, although understandable in terms of the high teacher–pupil ratio required, that the majority of the children in the first and second years, those not taking remedial reading or advanced literacy, did not receive a systematic exposure to reading practice of this kind.

World Studies

Even though the lower-school literacy scheme became the official lower-school language policy, the World Studies teachers, who were responsible for teaching the literacy scheme, had increasingly become interested in language and learning proper. A very brief account of some aspects of their work is included here to indicate where that work seemed to be heading and to illustrate the department's awareness of its own need to change.

First- and second-years at School 4 had eight periods of World Studies (in mixed-ability groups). In terms of traditional curriculum subjects the course covered English, History and Geography. The decision about what should be taught on the integrated course, apart from the need to harness the knowledge and skills of the teachers involved, was to some extent influenced by practices in feeder primary schools. Many of the 11-year-olds coming to the school had already done considerable work on the local environment. This helped to determine the wide scope of the integrated syllabus which became World Studies. At the time of my visit the first-year syllabus dealt with: the Solar System, the earth's crust, mountains, volcanoes, earthquakes, atlas work, the water cycle, a journey down a river, evolution, the first man, hunting, hunting to farming, frozen lands, mountains (as habitation), equatorial forests and deserts. The second-year syllabus dealt with historical and geographical aspects of particular civilizations, India and China among them. Lower-school World Studies work had its own head of department, that is, although the course displaced English, Geography and History in the first two years, it was a separate department. As a result none of the contributing subjects was taught as it would have been if it had been taught separately, under the aegis of the heads of English, Geography or History, all of whom worked in the upper school.

Each week, on Monday after school, the World Studies team met to check on the work of the forthcoming week and to plan ahead. This was the opportunity for heads of department from the upper school to take an interest in what was going on in lower school. The Head of English, for instance, was a regular attender. The Head of World Studies, fairly recently appointed, was continually assessing the course as a whole. His main criticism of the course as he had found it was that it was 'too repetitious and too content-oriented', and indeed this is a common combination. A course which is set up as 'topics' or amounts of knowledge to get through is always in danger of leading to repetitious methodology, using chunks of stuff, usually pages from a book, to be read, absorbed, reproduced, ticked.

An important item in the weekly meeting was the regular lecture featured in each of the three years of the World Studies course. The main aim of the lecture was to enable pupils to listen, select and reconstruct skilfully, abilities which are largely taken for granted as developing

spontaneously in these years. Of course, on some level these comprehending activities do just happen whether or not we are, or have ever
been, in school. But this does not mean to say that it is therefore un-
necessary to encourage children to listen in particular ways in lessons.
Members of the World Studies team took turns to give the weekly lecture. The one I saw on earthquakes was typical, the teacher using an
overhead projector to show slides (diagrams of the earth's crust, photographs of earthquake damage) and to provide in writing the key pieces
of information featured. For instance, one item looked like this:

When an earthquake happens near the sea it causes huge waves called
Tsunami (Japanese word)   tsu   harbour
                          nami   waves.

The idea was that such lectures, usually given to half a year group at a
time, would provide a common core of information which everyone
could call upon and could take to other work done on the topic. Some of
the writing (indicated by colour on the overhead projector) would be
copied into special lecture notebooks for reference later. In the case of
the earthquake lecture there were a number of pieces of follow-up and
continuation work. One of these was a school-duplicated booklet, taking
the form of a series of questions following closely the material provided
in the lecture. Other work included looking at photographs of earthquakes in Alaska and Turkey and describing damage done, and answering a worksheet of questions on three pages of Macdonald's *Earthquakes, Volcanoes and Mountains*.[1] Some groups were provided with a
list of famous volcanoes and an atlas and had to find out where the
earthquakes were and mark them on an outline map, a fairly difficult
job entailing using an index precisely and transferring information
from an atlas map to an outline map on a different scale. Imaginative
work included a newspaper report of an earthquake in the South-East
London area, and an acrostic using the word 'earthquake'.

This sequence of work illustrated fairly succinctly the one-sided concentration on making and using notes that had developed at that stage.
The lecture and follow-up booklet (an exercise requiring the children to
use their own notes from the lecture to answer a series of questions) had
been produced with care and effort. But a disproportionate amount of
time was spent in class on the long comprehension exercises in the
follow-up booklet so that there did not seem to be time to discuss the
newspaper report-writing, which was left for homework. Although the
children were being asked to reconstruct in their imagination an experience of an earthquake, they were not being shown how they might con-

nect the large amounts of material they had been given with their imaginative work. Nor were techniques for report-writing discussed.

The topics themselves presented other difficulties in relation to language and learning. They were well and truly distant from the children's local environment, which implies distant from their language and experience – probably the greatest resources that teachers can call upon in showing children the way to new knowledge. I am not saying that therefore children should be taught only about their surroundings, but that a list of topics as remote as this one will present difficulties for the teacher wanting to build bridges between the familiar and the new. The Head of Humanities in School 1 had tackled this difficulty by basing her first years' study of a medieval village on their earlier studies of their own villages. The work she went on to do on village life in India was informed by the children's work on the two earlier topics.

At the time of my visit the Head of World Studies at School 4 was considering re-shaping the course to give English work a great emphasis. He proposed to devote a fortnight to fully integrated work, followed by a week in which English would be treated as a separate subject. It was a recognition, on his part, of the way in which the mass of content was dictating a working pattern which left little space for more creative, speculative activity such as the reading and writing of stories and poetry, indeed little space for the children to organize any of their own learning.

It would be a sad victory for language and learning if the new provision for English work were to mean that the rest of the World Studies course continued as a monolith of knowledge. The head of department felt that this need not happen. Already some good English work had been done. Small class libraries had been made; the department was collecting together those books which were sure winners as class readers; and because the library was physically in the centre of the World Studies area the children were visiting it and borrowing fiction.

For the rest of the course, the head of department appreciated that the emphasis in planning sessions must be shifted away from lectures and note-making towards devising activities and materials for work where pupils could, on their own or in small groups, make use of the factual content of the course in discussion and writing which was more in their charge.

Metalwork

One of the comments made in the report on the lower-school literacy programme by the ILEA's Research and Statistics Branch was that very few teachers seemed to have followed through one of the aspects of the programme: the provision of a list of key words used in particular subjects. There were, nevertheless, individual teachers who had not only taken the word list seriously but were imaginative about its place in the lessons. An illustration was provided by one metalwork/woodwork teacher.

On the wall of the metal workshop was a clearly displayed word list, a mixture of specialist metalwork words and words with a wider currency but which crop up frequently in metalwork lessons. The complete list was as follows:

design, draw, hole, rings, together, hexagon, cube, pyramid, tin plate, aluminium, brass, copper, wire, colour, jewellery, solder, enamel, metal, piece, mark, cut, file, bend, smooth, polish, shine, shape, texture, pattern, geometric, natural, square, circle, triangle.

On seeing this my interest was in how accurately and thoughtfully the children could use those words, how much they were a part of their understanding of metalwork. Asking two boys, in a mixed-ability group of first-year boys and girls, to tell me about what they had done in metalwork was very fruitful. The two of them consulted their folders to give an account of all the projects they had worked on so far. Project 2 involved designing and making a house number-plate. Alan, who had done most of the explaining for Project 1, pushed Danny into the foreground with: 'Here Danny, you explain that.'

DANNY You had to have a square of metal and then you had to draw a line between it with the scriber.
I.R. You had to draw a line what?
DANNY Between the metal with a scriber.
I.R. What's a scriber?
ALAN It's like a pencil but it's to mark metal.
DANNY It's like a sort of pointed pencil made of metal. Well, before that, though, you had to get a piece of paper and draw your number of your door on it and then –
ALAN – and you had to put it on that number.
DANNY You had to cut it out and put it on the piece of metal and cut the metal out.
I.R. So you cut the paper out . . .
BOTH Yes.
ALAN . . . put it on the metal, and when that dries you can cut round the paper. It will be easier and then it's forty by forty millimetres and –
I.R. It's what, forty by forty?
ALAN Millimetres, the number, and in the middle you use a piercing saw. You

get a centre punch that's to make a little hole, like that you can see there, and then you cut around it with a piercing saw.
I.R. Oh, yes.
DANNY We broke a lot of them, didn't we?
ALAN Yes, we broke a lot.

The account continued with the two of them explaining how the edges of the numbers were smoothed, then given a shine on the grinder by the teacher. After that, they explained, they polished their numbers and stuck them onto pieces of wood with a special glue (they checked with their teacher that this was Araldite, and told me that it comes in two tubes and has to be mixed). I appreciated the boys' account of their metalwork course, which they had been doing for just two months, because it was informed and because they were patient in telling and teaching me about it. I felt, for instance, that I could have had a fairly successful attempt at making a house number myself, just from having listened to them. They used their special words proudly, in the way that children do with special words, but also precisely.

The following week, most of the class was ready to begin a new project: designing and making a copper wristband with a textured pattern. It was time for the teacher to gather the group together to introduce the new work. A description of the project was already up on the blackboard and the first thing that the teacher did was to read this aloud to the class clearly and fairly slowly. The most difficult sentence was this: 'On part of the wristband you should have a textured design which is to be based on a shape developed from a square.' The teacher read it twice.

TEACHER Right, what is a texture?
   [*Pupils offer two wrong answers which the tape-recorder does not pick up clearly.*]
TEACHER No, go back to your first projects.
PUPIL Sir, it's symmetrical.
GIRL Sir, it's a pattern – a pattern –
   [*Other voices join in.*]
TEACHER All right, finish explaining.
GIRL Sir, it's all different patterns, it's a pattern.
BOY Sir, it's sort of a rough surface or a smooth surface.
GIRL Yes.
TEACHER It's a sort of rough surface or a smooth surface, so a texture is a surface pattern.
GIRL Yes, that's it.
TEACHER Now, in the first project, that was a textured triangle. We decorated the surface with a texture. Now what we're going to do this morning is use a texture to make the surface of a wristband more interesting.

'Developing a square' (unlike 'texture') was new to the group. The teacher spent considerable time on this idea. The class suggested that a square has four equal sides, four corners, four right angles. The teacher then demonstrated a developed square.

TEACHER All you've got to do is put a straight line somewhere through that square. We're now developing that square. We're changing its shape to something else, so let's put a very simple line through there. Now what I want you to do then is move one part, slide it along that line so [*demonstrates on board*], so that distance there should be the same as that distance there, so now this is your shape, so you've developed a square and it's now that shape. Right, so we say we've developed a square, changed the shape of the square into this design.

What was impressive about this part of the lesson was how much time and care was taken in preparing the group for their project and, particularly, the care given to language. There were many nicely handled little points, and it is often the small points which make good practice. For instance, the reading out of the blackboard notice twice was essential in a mixed-ability class in which a number of the children would not have been able to read the notice for themselves. When 'textured' (a term from their first projects, but not from their second) cropped up the class slowly and hesitantly remembered the word, with the teacher prodding the recollection along the right lines. His contribution struck me as particularly sensitive, because he was not just giving a quick definition, but was showing how the word is employed. The same skill was shown with 'developing', when how to develop a square and what it means to develop a square were dealt with clearly and cogently. At a later stage in the lesson the teacher demonstrated ways of filing to a number of groups. A piece of paper was wrapped around the metal being filed in the vice:

TEACHER What do you think the bit of paper is for?
VOICE 1 Because where they've got little silver spikes, and when they crush it, it makes a funny pattern on it, sir.
VOICE 2 What?
VOICE 1 It's got little, er, things sticking out.
VOICE Patterns, sir.
TEACHER Whats?
VOICE Textured pattern.
TEACHER There's a sort of textured surface on the inside of the vice. So to protect your piece of metal you put a piece of paper round it.

The children were encouraged to see another occasion for using the word 'texture'. As these examples demonstrate, this teacher had used his word list not simply as a means to the naming of parts or defining terms but he had also consistently taken care to build up contexts in which the words were used meaningfully in his own demonstrations and explanations.

At the end of each project members of the class were asked to write up a report of what they had done. Alan's and Danny's (uncorrected) reports on their first project revealed interesting differences in their work.

Alan's work

Cut out an equilateral triangle from the metel provided (tinplate, aliminium, brass, copper). Design a symetrical shape to fit inside, one half is to be *posative* and the other negative. Size 100 mm.

Project 1
Write how you marked, cut, filed, and textured your equalateral triangle.

point 1 We marked out 50 mm on our metal with the ruler
point 2 We got our divider and marked out our three main points
point 3 We joined the three main points together and put a line the the middle using our try square and scriber
point 4 We put in the triangle our symetrical pattern and then we textured it with centre punch
point 5 We filed down the corners and then Mr H polished it with the grinder and then we polished it with some polish
point 6 We filed the edges to the where equal
point 7 We banged the triangle with the wooden mallet so it was all flat.

Danny's Work

Write how you marked, cut, filed and textured your equilateral triangle.

1. First you got ruler and dividers and a scriber
2. The you dun a 50 mm triangle
3. And then you slide it
4. Then you drawed the axis
5. Then you dun your patan
6. The you got a leter punch or a punch and make patan holes in it
7. And then you varnish it.

It isn't just that Alan is more technically accurate and that he obviously finds writing less burdensome than Danny. His written work also displays the explicitness of his talk. A reader can get a very good idea of how to make a patterned triangle from his account. Danny's work, on the other hand, gives the reader a hard time.

The organization of appropriate written work in metal design and other craft lessons could well become a productive area for discussion. For instance, the Home Economics teacher in School 3 was considering getting her small groups of pupils to plan writing together, just as they discussed questions and made oral reports together. A parallel move in the Metalwork Department in School 4 would be a good way into language across the curriculum work. This is not to criticize what is already going on there – the opposite, in fact – but to remind the reader of points I raise elsewhere in this account: the failure so far of the language policy committee to encourage the sort of exploration of language in the classroom which I have attempted to sketch here, and the lack of a sustained commitment to language and learning in the school. Hopefully the committee could develop as School 1's group did (for the two committees were similarly constituted), to provide a forum for expanding such useful work as this, which could otherwise easily go unacknowledged.

Prospects for future policies

School 4's language working group had a brief to survey language in the school and make recommendations. The school's official policy document was an outcome of this work. But, as the committee's report to Academic Committee (Appendix D) shows, they lost touch with what had happened to the recommendations and with what was going on in departments. The new committee, chosen by department to represent their interests, now had the job of collecting and disseminating ideas as well as the inevitable one of learning for themselves about language across the curriculum. The first sign of a direct influence came from the lower-school World Studies team, who produced a paper on note-making in response to the committee's considerations. However uncertain one might feel about this area as a priority for the World Studies course, it was a document that could well benefit other departments.

Shortly before my visit, as part of a revival of interest in language and learning, the Mathematics Department produced a maths dictionary. This was fifteen sturdily bound A4 sides of mathematical words. Meanings were given, often with illustrations and diagrams. The dictionary was not just another example of those lists of key words which, when devised, had largely been ignored (the metalwork I saw being an impressive exception). It encapsulated a recognition that the technical and initially unfamiliar terms of mathematics could be daunting, but that their meanings could be given in more familiar language. For instance the entry 'ellipse' had a diagram of an ellipse and the definition 'squashed circle'. A child using such a dictionary could overcome some of the frustration of not understanding mathematics because of not understanding the words in which it was articulated.

But there are, I feel, difficulties in the way of success. As I mention in all the case studies, a commitment expressed by the leadership of a school is essential to the success of language policy work. The head needs to give his or her support to language and learning and recognize it as a curriculum issue, delegating the responsibility for it and, more importantly, providing the time for that responsibility to be taken on. I feel that this was not appreciated at School 4. The Director of Studies, who has the onerous job of consulting with heads of department and producing a timetable (which takes up most of his time for the entire summer term), cannot realistically be asked in a school as large as this to take on the responsibility for curriculum development, too. Whoever is in charge of language across the curriculum must on the one hand have the vision to recognize that language in teaching is not an educational fad to be dropped when the fashion changes and when, say, standards come into vogue; and, on the other, he or she must have available the time and energy to insist that language across the curriculum stays alive.

There is a point, too, to be made about the general direction that language and learning had taken in the school. Up to the time of my study, it had not seemed to be about what goes on in ordinary lessons. This can be partly accounted for by remembering that language across the curriculum at this school must be regarded first and foremost as to do with basic reading and writing. As I have indicated, literacy, in timetable terms and in the eyes of the children, had become another school subject. This was getting in the way of seeing language and learning as to do with the learning via language of pupils of all abilities in all subjects. There had not yet been a discussion in depth of what reading and writing have to do with learning.

References

1. Roger Clare, *Earthquakes, Volcanoes and Mountains*, Macdonald Educational, 1971.

VI. Conclusion

The changes in educational thinking and practice which are reported in the preceding case studies do not lend themselves to the formulation of definitive results or findings. This book will have achieved its main aim if the reader has been able to build up an impression of what 'language across the curriculum' might look like in action. At the same time there emerge from the studies fairly clear indications of the circumstances enabling language policy to work in schools and a number of warnings about difficulties. These are summarized here.

Responsibility for language policy
 i The head needs to recognize language policy as his or her direct responsibility and needs to delegate at a suitably senior level, in recognition of the importance of the work.
 ii A sustained commitment by the head's delegate seems vital for the success of a language policy. The commitment may be a very active one (as in Schools 1 and 2) or it may take the form of providing timetabled space (as in School 3) to enable the work to go ahead.

Working parties
If a language committee or working party is to remain in touch with the staff as a whole, and if its recommendations are to carry weight, then it should probably be formed from members elected by the departments and responsible for reporting back to them. Once established, however, the working party will need time for members to learn from each other and to educate themselves in the ramifications of language across the curriculum. The problem of finding the right balance between self-education and the preparation and following through of recommendations to other teachers taxed all of the committees studied in this report to one degree or another, and will need careful attention wherever systematic language work is first undertaken.

Many working parties begin their lives by organizing large-scale activities to launch language across the curriculum in their schools. Only too often these events (such as surveys, which I have discussed in Chapter IV) take up enormous amounts of time and energy and succeed in generating as much suspicion and even hostility as they do interest and enthusiasm. The best work I saw consisted in teachers monitoring their own activities – listening to themselves giving instructions or setting up lessons, looking critically at the textbooks they were putting in front of children – and those of their pupils at work in groups. Once we recognize that language across the curriculum is all about this process of monitoring, analysing and modifying our own practices, then finding a starting point is not difficult.

It is harder to decide at what stage one should look at practice in the light of the many writings about language and learning. The question is often posed as: At what stage should we introduce theoretical perspectives? This is to look at the problem in the wrong way. All activity has a theoretical base, explicit or implicit; the objective is to bring the assumptions which underlie our teaching methods out into the open so that they can be examined and, where necessary, changed. When we are aware of the difference in our own practice between genuinely inviting children to learn and simply getting them to absorb or reproduce given facts, then we can begin to assemble the pedagogic principles for encouraging the one and discouraging the other. Theoretical writings about language across the curriculum will usually be of greatest help in formulating and generalizing these principles.

Outside assistance
   i The most effective help from outside agencies appears to be the kind which comes in small, regular doses. The effects of such help in School 3 were impressive. Teachers who read this may well feel that they could never find such help. However, they could bear in mind the effectiveness of continued support when they decide either to go on a week-long course, say, or to persuade their teachers' centre to put on a series of meetings over a longer period period of time.
   ii No course or outside agency can replace the bread-and-butter work of monitoring and reflecting upon one's own practices.
  iii Bearing in mind that language policy will be asking a lot of working party members, secretarial help should be provided. No one should be two-finger typing minutes or reports. Such help would be an index of a head's commitment to language policy.

Language across the curriculum and subject areas
As we have seen throughout the case studies, language policy work

has generally been carried out with mixed-ability classes, or in integrated courses, and has tended to be confined to the junior years of secondary schools.

Examination syllabuses at 16+, exerting as they do considerable pressure to 'cover the ground', seem to prevent most people from shifting the emphasis of work with older pupils from the content to be dealt with to a concern with the processes of learning and teaching highlighted in the case studies. Examination syllabuses are typically presented as lists of topics to be studied and are an implicit invitation to see knowledge as 'fact'. Indeed, most written examination papers do little more than invite regurgitation. One way of avoiding the pressure is to establish Mode III syllabuses (organized and assessed within school) which would emphasize learning as process not as product.

The role of the English Department

As the Bullock Report's elucidation of language across the curriculum ('the role of language in other areas of the curriculum than English') might be thought to imply that a school's English Department has no special contribution to make to a language policy, it is important to establish what this departmental contribution might be.

English is often thought of as a 'service subject' in relation to other departments, providing children with skills such as the ability to spell, summarize or write clear descriptions which they will then transfer and use in other more content-centred subjects. In reality, English teachers can offer colleagues in other disciplines their practical experience of drawing on the language talents latent in children by suggesting a variety of ways of setting them tasks. This collaborative approach is likely to be more effective than one which focuses on an attempt to equip pupils with 'basic skills'. Making children effective writers of stories or poems is not a self-indulgent occupation of no use to learning in other departments. It involves pupils in vital practice at handling their own learning and modifying its expression themselves.

The emphasis placed in some schools (cf. p. 35) on 'language exercise' – spelling, grammar, précis, synonyms, cognate verb/adjective/noun forms – often assume that there is some key set of language abilities which must come, in a child's learning, before being able to write effectively. Recognizing that technical competence in the formalities of orthography, syntax and style is related in a much more complex way to being able to get things done through reading and writing is one route to the realization that all departments have something to add to the growth of language across the curriculum.

Appendices

Appendix A Report on the homework survey at School 3

I

The 'Bullock' Committee was asked by the Curriculum Development Committee to explore the homework policy of the school. There were anxieties that in the third year:

(a) Pupils were not being given enough experience of the kind of work they would be expected to do in the fourth year.
(b) Not enough demands were being made on the pupils. They were not being extended.
(c) Staff might not be setting homework as often as the policy handbook and the timetable indicated.

II

The 'Bullock' Committee set out to explore these questions by collecting evidence of the amount and the varieties of homework actually done. The first attempt was to examine homework notebooks, but it was found that they were rarely used.

A specific project was therefore begun with a third-year tutor group. The girls were asked to note all homework over the period of three weeks, to time the work set during one week and to indicate the type of homework.

The specific questions the Committee were trying to answer were:

1. How much homework is supposed to be set per week? How much is actually set?
2. What types of homework were set?
3. How long does it take the girls to do it?
4. Why do teachers actually set homework?

III

The accompanying Table 1 shows the amount of homework set. Since the groups contain sets in some subjects, there is more than the basic 14 units multiplied by 3.

The descriptions of the varieties of homework in Table 1 are based on the descriptions in the homework notebooks. They are presented in order of frequency of occurrence during the three weeks. There is little evidence to suggest that different abilities are set different types of homework.

For comparison Table 2 shows a sample of fourth-year homework set in one week.

Average time spent on homework: 5 hours 36 mins.
Maximum time spent on homework: 9 hours.
Minimum time spent on homework: 1 hour 50 mins.

Table 1 Third-year homework over three weeks

Type of homework set	Week 1	Week 2	Week 3	Total
None	6	8	6	20
Finish off	3	4	4	11
Revise	2	5	4	11
Copy up	3	3	–	6
None – teacher absent	2	3	1	6
Project	2	2	2	6
Problems	1	2	1	4
Written questions	1	1	1	3
Collect (e.g. words, materials)	1	1	2	4
Research	–	1	2	3
Rough work	–	1	1	2
Draw and label	1	–	1	2
Poster work	1	1	–	2
Read	–	–	1	1
Read and comprehend	–	–	1	1
Essay	–	–	1	1
Think about	–	–	1	1
Image	–	1	–	1

Table 2   Fourth-year homework over one week

Type	Total
No homework	21
Finish off	12
Copy up notes	10
Answer questions (in writing)	10
Essay	9
Written notes	7
Problems	6
Project	4
Copy up experiment	4
Read	4
Revise	4
Drawings	2
None – teacher absent	2
Exercises (in French)	1
Learn (= memorize)	1
List examples	1
Check dictation	1

There were some discrepancies between the length of time that homework is supposed to take (7 hours per week according to the third-year timetable) and the actual time it took. The times are as follows:

Average time teachers estimated: 4 hours 23 mins.
Average time actually spent: 5 hours 22 mins.
The longest time spent on homework: 12 hours 5 mins.

Further investigation could be done to see whether the length of time pupils take over their homework relates in any way to the attainment level that the pupils achieve.

We have insufficient information to answer the question, 'Why do teachers set homework?'

IV

The group tutor discussed with the pupils their own and their parents' reaction to homework. Several interesting points were made, falling into the following general areas:

Area 1. The majority of pupils have many very worth-while out-of-school activities. These include music lessons, speech training, guides, girls' brigade, youth club, gym club (not school), pony care and discos. They consequently prefer to have homework set within sufficient time before it is to be handed in, so that they can plan it to fit in with their other commitments. This is difficult in some subjects. It seems that those who attend regular evening activities do their homework at weekends, and parent reaction is that if it can all be done at the weekends then not enough homework is being set.

Conversely, girls with few evening activities regularly attempt homework most evenings, take longer over it (presumably because they're not committed elsewhere), and parent reaction is that too much is set.

Some parents have considered phoning in to school but don't in case they are thought of as interfering or trouble-making. Some parents insist the girls stop work at 9 or 9.30 p.m. whether they've finished or not.

Area 2. There seem to be two reasons why homework can sometimes take $1\frac{1}{2}$–2 hours longer than either the homework timetable suggests or the teacher estimates. Firstly, it happens when the particular subject teacher aims to get through a vast amount of factual work in a lesson. He/she writes notes on the blackboard which girls have to rapidly scribble down. They then rewrite neatly at home, often having to look up points to fill in the blanks. Secondly, when tasks include such things as:

'Imagine you have met a spaceman, try to describe the shops which are unknown to him. Write a story about this.' (Home Economics homework)

'Do a newspaper clip on the trail or when they come home. Do it like a proper newspaper. Do questions 1, 2, 3, 5 as well.' (History homework)

This type of work, which is desirable because it demands more than straightforward reiteration of facts, none the less increases the time taken, especially when set to less able girls.

Area 3. Revision and learning homework seem to be most distressing to the girls. Little guidance is given as to how to do this. Staff seem to imply it is the complete responsibility of the pupil with instructions being to:

'Take 2–3 hours or as long as you need to ensure that you know it well.'

Area 4. Project work too seems to need a special mention. It would seem that some staff will set a project to be completed during a holiday time and give no prior help with either the subject or how to compile a project.

V

The survey and the discussions we have had raised several complex questions. We have found to our surprise that talking about a subject as apparently mundane as homework has led us into heated arguments and intense discussion and has raised quite fundamental issues about teaching in general. We identify four key areas:

(a) the form and variety of homework provided;
(b) the effectiveness of homework for assisting learning;
(c) teachers' attitudes and policies; and
(d) effects of homework on child and parent.

Some attempt has been made to consider area (d) – see section IV. The other areas include many important questions which are unanswered and which the Committee does not feel competent to answer. We suggest that areas (a) and (c) contain the following specific points:

Area (a)
(i) length of time between setting and handing in;
(ii) recognition by staff of how long homework will take;
(iii) setting of a greater variety of homework;
(iv) difference between homework timetable and number of homeworks set;
(v) planning of homework with more regard to mixed ability;
(vi) vacation work.

Area (c)
(i) marking of homework;
(ii) teachers' reasons for setting homework;
(iii) department policy;
(iv) use of the homework notebooks.

VI

We also considered the original statement made in the staff handbook. The following points seem relevant:

1. Of the five defined functions for homework, 'finishing class work' seems dominant. There seems to be little evidence (in our survey) to suggest homework is used for exploring, finding out or for reflective writing.
2. Although staff intended to establish a habit of independent work, the pupils (and their parents) often do not share their feelings. This may be because of the homework set, which, being largely 'finishing off' and 're-vision', does not seem particularly attractive to the pupils nor indeed to encourage this habit.
3. Although the handbook appears to identify good practice with regard to homework, it may well be that staff would wish to re-examine what constitutes good practice.
4. The handbook's statement, which is the result of earlier staff discussion, is quite explicit about the setting of homework. A department may choose to

opt out of the homework timetable in the lower and middle school. However, the handbook continues quite explicitly: 'If a department asks for a preparation commitment then work must be set, except on the very rare occasions when nothing meaningful can be given.'

It seems clear to us that either the handbook statement must be altered to take account of actual practice, or departments should consider very carefully what has happened to take them away from a statement they themselves have made and agreed to.

VII

We wish to propose that discussions be held to consider some of these questions. In particular, we recommend as a matter of urgency that when 'revision' homework is set the department should explain to pupils how to set about revising and what it involves.

Among the unanswered questions, the Committee feel that the following require special consideration:

What does a department hope will be the results of its homework policy?

Are these desired results actually achieved? For instance, if the function of homework is for pupils to remember something, do they actually remember it? If not, how can a department help pupils to remember?

Appendix B Part of an amendment to the school handbook of School 3

Where departments need homework it should be seen as part of the syllabus and planned within the scheme of work. It should never be a constraint on the lesson, and its effectiveness can only be judged in conjunction with the effectiveness of the lesson. It enables the teacher to ensure that in lesson time the pupil can derive maximum benefit from her peers and her teachers. Teachers must ensure that girls understand the way they are to carry out their homework tasks, and these should be within the capabilities of individual children (not easy to set in a mixed-ability class). It should establish the habit of independent work.

PURPOSE AND TYPES OF HOMEWORK
   A feedback for comprehension and a measure of the depth of understanding of work already covered.
   Reinforcement of concepts, ideas and methods.
   Research (teachers must ensure girls do not just copy up).
   Learning.
   Reading.
   Talking with the family or friends.

(The last three are so valuable that the risk that some will not do it should be taken.)

   Preparation for practical work.
   Collecting material for the next lesson or homework.
   Making progress in a task to maintain interest.

ROUTINE WRITING CAN BE COUNTER-PRODUCTIVE

Heads of department are responsible for studying and rationalizing the marking programme. Each department should have its clearly defined practice which is explained to the girls.

Appendix C Reading section of School 4's language policy document

1. *What do we mean by reading?*

Each one of us, pupil and teacher alike, is at a particular stage in learning to read. Contrary to popular assumption, reading is not a skill which we suddenly acquire; it is, rather, a continuing, developmental process.

When we say that a child is a poor reader, perhaps most of us mean that he has not mastered the formal techniques, the mechanics of recognition, that he cannot decode the symbols on the page in front of him. This, for all its difficulties, is just the basic prerequisite for reading. Deciphering the squiggles is futile without understanding what they mean; individual words must be grouped together into phrases, sentences and paragraphs, so that a factual account, a set of instructions, an argument or a story can be followed. Awareness of mood and tone, response to the author's attitudes, and the ability to differentiate between fact and opinion, and indeed between biased and objective opinion, are more sophisticated reading skills. Perhaps we do not give enough consideration to the different activities which are disguised under the blanket term 'reading'. Reading a novel demands a different response from reading a holiday brochure or a railway timetable; different levels of our awareness are involved when we read Agatha Christie and when we read Tolstoy.

2. *Reading in the curriculum*

Reading is essential for most subjects in the curriculum. For some, it is vital; for others, notably some of the arts and crafts subjects, it is of limited importance and is not part of the child's expectations. Even so, there are opportunities for reading and a capable reader can gain greater insight into these subjects. Other practical subjects, and most non-practical ones, consider reading to be important. It obviously has great significance as far as examinations are concerned.

3. *The reading we demand*

Children are required to read:

> textbooks, library books (non-fiction)
> reference books
> magazines
> teacher-prepared notes or information sheets
> wallcharts
> from the blackboard
> lists of specialist words
> books, library books (fiction)
> worksheets, workcards
> examination papers.

They are asked, either as a class or as individuals to:

(a) read instructions;
(b) read, understand, extract and use information. This seems to be the greatest single function of reading in the curriculum. Many activities, like answering worksheets or making notes, obviously involve both reading and writing, and sometimes other skills as well. It is perhaps time that we looked at the function of worksheets; it is sometimes possible for answers to be elicited from the text without any real reading, in the sense of understanding, having taken place;
(c) read for pleasure. It must be said, however, that with our emphasis on content and specialist subjects, there is limited opportunity for children to choose the material they want to read and to read for its own sake. The obvious exception is the English lesson.

4. *Specialist vocabulary*
Nearly all subjects have their own terminology. Some terms are new to the children; others are in common use but have a definite, precise meaning in a particular subject. Teachers are aware that specialist language, which should clarify or particularize an idea or a process in an economic way, can often be a potential barrier to understanding; there is a gulf between the teacher's terms of reference and those of his pupils. Teachers see that teaching the language of a subject is part of their job and have devised various methods of doing this. Even when pupils can read the vocabulary of a subject, however, they often fail to reproduce it with accuracy or understanding in subsequent talk or writing.

We would recommend that departments

(a) examine the extent to which they use specialist terminology;
(b) consider what is essential, and must be retained, and what could be replaced by 'ordinary' language, without loss to the subject;
(c) work out a regular, continuous programme to ensure that the children can read, understand, write and spell the terms they deem essential.

Children can be exposed to such 'core' vocabulary by

(i) having wallcharts available;
(ii) making lists themselves from the board, OHP, etc., and having to learn them for homework;
(iii) having flashcards in the classroom for use at odd moments;
(iv) having spelling tests;
(v) constant repetition on the part of the teacher.

5. *Gauging the difficulty of reading material*
We felt that most samples of reading material given to us by departments were too difficult for the majority of children. In preparing or choosing material, the following considerations are important:

(a) The amount of new information or vocabulary presented at any one time should be limited. The child should know as much as possible about the text before reading it or before it is read to him, so that he knows what to expect and can adjust his frames of reference accordingly. Where the vocabulary and concepts are familiar, the task is the comparatively simple one of recognition and association. Where the reader is not familiar with the information he has to read – where a new topic is introduced through reading or where he has to make notes on his own, for example – the demands are much greater. The reader has no experience to draw on and cannot therefore gain clues from the context. Even if he can decipher the symbols on the page, there is no guarantee of his being able to understand or use them. A sophisticated adult reader can be presented with information on a subject about which he knows nothing, can 'read' it and be none the wiser. Reading without understanding leads to frustration; how many of us have discarded an article or book because the first paragraph was too difficult?

(b) Sentence length and the number of syllables per word are some guide in gauging how difficult a text will be. Multi-syllabic words are usually, though not always, harder to read than words with few syllables. Likewise, sentence length usually, though not always, correlates with prose complexity.

(c) The presentation of material can also help or hinder reading.

(i) There could, perhaps, be greater uniformity throughout the school in teachers' use of capital and lower-case letters; quite apart from the conventions we expect the children to adhere to in their own writing, poor readers have difficulty in reading texts comprised entirely of capital letters.

(ii) Sub-headings break up the text. They can direct attention, show a logical sequence, help a reader 'pace' his concentration when he has lapsed to get back into the text.

(iii) Adequate summaries at strategic points in the text help the pupil to consolidate what he has just read before moving on to new information.

(iv) Accompanying diagrams and pictures provide clues to the reader and should be used alongside texts where appropriate.

(v) Texts should be legible. Type is usually easier for children to read than is teachers' handwriting, as used on banda sheets, for example. There should be adequate spacing between lines. Poor readers have less difficulty with large print.

6. *Who does the reading?*
Mostly commonly, the teacher reads to the class or the pupil reads alone. Understandably, pupils on the whole prefer the teacher to do the reading. After all, in writing, unlike speech, there is no stress or pitch to help us understand what someone means, and the signals (punctuation) are for the eye alone. Even factual prose, which does not need to be read with the expression and interpretation we reserve for fiction, may therefore cause difficulty if pupils are expected to read on their own.

7. *Reading aloud*
Over several years the English Department has found that many of the children enjoy reading aloud. There is a persistent demand for plays for this reason. Surprisingly, a significant number of children who ask to read aloud are those whom we would consider to be below average readers. Leaving aside the children's preference for fast narrative drama, and leaving aside those children who

want to read aloud in order to boost their ego, the demand remains.

It has also been found that many children like to read their own or other pupils' writing onto tape.

As teachers, perhaps we avoid giving the opportunity for this to happen right across the curriculum – mostly because we want the text to be read 'correctly' or because we are timid about choosing a pupil who will be ashamed because he is unable to cope.

There are a number of advantages to reading aloud:

(a) it involves the pupils much more in the lesson;
(b) it goes part of the way to transferring the responsibility to read to the pupil;
(c) it enables the teacher to see clearly where textual difficulties are greatest.

Obviously such practice will not always be appropriate, and compelling a pupil to read aloud in public would be insensitive teaching – but we would suggest that asking for voluntary readers, splitting a large chunk of text between several pupils, thanking pupils for doing it, and intervening tactfully to help and summarize, will probably be beneficial to both class and teacher.

8. *The common-core vocabulary*

Finally – on a note of simplicity – there are about 200 words which we all use extensively. Surely, as a school, we can at least find ways of ensuring that each child can read, and also write and spell, this limited vocabulary which *is* within his understanding.

We would recommend that:

(a) a greater demand should be put on the children to read (there will always be a place for the teacher reading some of the time);
(b) if we agree with (a) above, then we must provide texts suitable for the levels of the pupils we teach;
(c) where children are asked to read on their own, they should be given an expectation of what they will meet, as it has been found that they cope better when this occurs. One way of doing this is for the teacher to give a brief summary of what is to be read.

Appendix D Statement on language policy presented to School 4's Academic Committee

Development of the language policy

The language policy in print was accepted by the staff. It is seen as (a) offering advice; (b) analysing the predominant modes of language in use in the school; (c) recommending certain language areas for special attention and development.

Since the policy was adopted, it has been virtually impossible to know to what extent it is being put into practice by any individual colleague or department. Nor is there any plan by which future developments can be monitored. We do not know how far colleagues have developed any of the recommendations on spelling, sentences, handwriting, reading, note-making/taking, essay work, worksheets or talk. We *do* know that the literacy scheme is still in operation in Lower School, as are the handwriting sessions, and that World Studies has compiled various spelling lists and are laying down a set pattern for teaching them. The English Department have done some groundwork on reading comprehension tasks and teaching the skills of extracting information and summary, etc. We are sure that other departments must be doing bits and pieces – but who knows?

We feel that no department can operate *all* aspects of the policy, but we would like to encourage as much effective practice as possible.

We feel also that the four of us who co-ordinated all the information and wrote the policy should now step down to make way for a more effective organization of everyone's efforts. We feel that all colleagues should have the opportunity of sharing development work on the policy and that some kind of organization should be established for this to happen.

We would like the Academic Committee to consider the following suggestions:

1. New teachers in the school should be introduced to the language policy as suggested in the final section of the policy.
2. Occasional talks by colleagues in the school and by visitors should be arranged by the Director of Studies. Hopefully these talks would be on particular points in the policy.
3. English and Remedial Reading Departments could always be available to attend panel meetings of any department which felt an 'outsider' could be helpful.
4. Some aspect of the policy should be a regular item on the agenda of departmental meetings.
5. Each department in the school should select one particular recommendation from the policy and develop and practise it over the next twelve months, with a view to reporting back to a standing committee (see No. 6).
6. There should be a standing committee called the Language Policy Committee. It should consist of representatives from *every* area of the curriculum and should be open to any colleague to attend. It should meet three times a year, and be covered by the Director of Studies. Its brief should be to hear reports from departments on development work, receive materials and pro-

vide occasional reports to the Head and the staff in order that colleagues might benefit from each other's work. This committee should also co-ordinate future developments for implementing the policy.

Further reading

Douglas Barnes, *From Communication to Curriculum*, Penguin, 1979.
Teachers interested in classroom talk as an effective learning medium will find this book useful as it demonstrates through various transcriptions the importance of talk.

James Britton, *Language and Learning*, Allen Lane, 1970 (now also available in Penguin).
This is an important book for it collects together, for teachers, understandings about language and learning and their relevance to educational practice.

Department of Education and Science, *A Language for Life*: Report of the Committee of Inquiry appointed by the Secretary of State for Education and Science under the Chairmanship of Sir Alan Bullock FBA, HMSO, 1975, Chapters 9, 10, 11, 12.
These chapters on literature, oral language, written language and language across the curriculum are the most relevant and helpful.

Nancy Martin, Pat D'Arcy, Bryan Newton and Robert Parker, *Writing and Learning Across the Curriculum 11–16*, Ward Lock Educational, 1976.
This is the report of the Schools Council Writing Across the Curriculum Project, which investigated the writing of secondary-school pupils in a number of subjects. The authors suggest that too much of the writing and talking in school is used to test what children know and too little is concerned with enabling them to learn and make sense of things for themselves.

The Schools Council team responsible for this book also produced a number of discussion pamphlets which, not least because of their brevity and conciseness, are excellent starters. These are: *Language and Learning in the Humanities, Writing in Science, From Information to Understanding, From Talking to Writing, Keeping Options Open, Why Write?* and *Language Policies in Schools: Aspects and Approaches.*

Frank Smith, *Reading*, Cambridge University Press, 1978.
This important writer's thesis is that children best learn to read by reading. The teacher's job becomes, then, assisting a child in learning to read rather than teaching reading. This book is a sound introduction to Smith's work.

Andrew Stibbs, *Assessing Children's Language: Guidelines for Teachers*, Ward Lock in association with the National Association for Teaching English, 1979.

The booklet moves from looking at everyday practices as assessors of children's language, through a series of more testing procedures, to a discussion of how we can most effectively assess in order to help children, rather than to point out that they have gone wrong.

Michael Stubbs, *Language, Schools and Classrooms*, Methuen, 1976.

This is a review of sociolinguistics as applied to the classroom. It is careful and thorough, and provides a good introduction to the work of, amongst others, Basil Bernstein.

Members of the Consultative Committee

C. Harrison (*Chairman*)	Lecturer, School of Education, Nottingham University
A. Adams	Lecturer, Department of Education, University of Cambridge
Ms. L. Barua	Teacher, Tile Hill Wood School, Coventry
T. Burgess	Lecturer, Institute of Education, University of London
Ms. A. Davey	Teacher, North Manchester High School, Lancashire
C. Elliott	Adviser, Hertfordshire
D. Goddard	Warden, Enfield Teachers' Centre, Middlesex
M. James	Deputy Headmaster, Toot Hill School, Nottinghamshire
M. Marland CBE	Headmaster, Woodberry Down School, London N4
J. Pratt	Teacher, Bushfield Community School, Peterborough
H. Gardiner (*Assessor*)	Senior Inspector for English, HM Inspectorate

Schools Council staff

Ms. H. Carter	Curriculum Officer
Ms. J. Nicoll	Research Officer